Launch:
Starting a New Church from Scratch

My dear friends Nelson and Kerrick have written a real winner about church planting. I am so proud of these guys. They are not theorists but veteran church planters who have successfully planted purpose-driven churches. Listen and learn from these gifted men! My prayer is that God will use this book to raise up another wave of new churches to reach a new generation that will serve God's purposes.

RICK WARREN
Author, *The Purpose Driven Church* and *The Purpose Driven Life*
Pastor, Saddleback Church
Lake Forest, California

Nelson Searcy and Kerrick Thomas are not ivory-tower theorists. They have launched a great church successfully, and now they have written a practical road map for others. Save yourself $100,000 and three years of your life . . . read *Launch*.

STEVE STROOPE
Author, *Money Matters in Church*
Senior Pastor, Lake Pointe Church
Rockwell, Texas

The day of "planting" new churches is gone. The day of "launching" new churches is here! No one in the world has a better grip on what that means than Nelson Searcy and Kerrick Thomas. Nelson is the best church strategist I know, and he excels even more in how to launch new churches.

DAN SOUTHERLAND
Author, *Transitions: Leading Your Church Through Change*
Lead Pastor, Next Level Church
Matthews, North Carolina

Nelson Searcy and Kerrick Thomas draw on their success at The Journey to bring us a much needed and practical field guide to church planting. *Launch: Starting a Church from Scratch* will be required reading for all church planters and new campus pastors at Seacoast Church in the future.

GEOFF SURRATT
Co-author, *The Multi-site Church Revolution*
Teaching Pastor, Seacoast Church
Columbia, South Carolina

I always find the musings of Nelson Searcy and Kerrick Thomas to be winsome, insightful and workable in the real world. This book once again confirms my expectations. It's got what you need to know and how you're going to feel when you launch a new church nailed down in a highly accessible format. Read it and get started!

LARRY OSBORNE
Pastor, North Coast Church and
The North Coast Training Network
Vista, California

Nelson Searcy is one of the most creative and gifted church planters I've ever met. It has been a joy for my church to participate as a partner with him in launching The Journey, the church Nelson pastors in New York City. I'm sure that the kingdom of Christ will greatly benefit from the helpful insight he and Kerrick Thomas share in *Launch: Starting a New Church from Scratch*.

BRYANT WRIGHT
Senior Pastor
Johnson Ferry Baptist Church
Marietta, Georgia

Launch

Starting a New Church from Scratch

Nelson Searcy
and Kerrick Thomas

Regal

From Gospel Light
Ventura, California, U.S.A.

PUBLISHED BY REGAL BOOKS
FROM GOSPEL LIGHT
VENTURA, CALIFORNIA, U.S.A.
PRINTED IN THE U.S.A.

Regal Books is a ministry of Gospel Light, a Christian publisher dedicated to serving the local church. We believe God's vision for Gospel Light is to provide church leaders with biblical, user-friendly materials that will help them evangelize, disciple and minister to children, youth and families.

It is our prayer that this Regal book will help you discover biblical truth for your own life and help you meet the needs of others. May God richly bless you.

For a free catalog of resources from Regal Books/Gospel Light, please call your Christian supplier or contact us at 1-800-4-GOSPEL *or* www.regalbooks.com.

Library of Congress Cataloging-in-Publication Data
Searcy, Nelson.
  Launch : starting a new church from scratch / Nelson Searcy, Kerrick Thomas.
    p. cm.
  ISBN 0-8307-4310-3 (trade paper)
  1. Church development, New. I. Thomas, Kerrick. II. Title.
  BV652.24.S43 2006
  254'.1—dc22   2006027802

  4   5   6   7   8   9   10   /   10   09   08   07

Rights for publishing this book in other languages are contracted by Gospel Light Worldwide, the international nonprofit ministry of Gospel Light. Gospel Light Worldwide also provides publishing and technical assistance to international publishers dedicated to producing Sunday School and Vacation Bible School curricula and books in the languages of the world. For additional information, visit www.gospellightworldwide.org; write to Gospel Light Worldwide, P.O. Box 3875, Ventura, CA 93006; or send an e-mail to info@gospellightworldwide.org.

Nelson: To Kelley, my wife and my best friend.
Thank you for taking a risk on our first blind date and for
saying yes to the hundreds of risks since, including moving to
New York City to start a church from scratch. And to our new
son, Alexander, whose adventure in life is just beginning.
My love for both of you grows every day.

Kerrick: To my wife and partner in ministry, Lorie,
who was courageous enough to move with me in the summer
of 2001 to a tiny, mouse-infested, one-room New York City
apartment in the East Village to try to start a church when
not a lot of people thought it was a great idea. And to my
mom . . . who thought it was a great idea all along.

Nelson and Kerrick would both like to thank the amazing
staff, members, volunteers and partners of The Journey
Church, our incredible editor Jennifer Henson, and the
committed staff of Regal Publishing for their partnership
and commitment to this project.

Contents

Section 1: Foundation

Section 2: Formation

Section 3: Implementation

Appendices

When I was in college, I took a life-changing course that had nothing to do with my major: art education. Literally every day of that semester, the beatnik-holdover professor, who dressed like someone plucked right out of Greenwich Village circa 1962, pounded on this simple idea: "If your art isn't practical, then it's good for nothing!" That was a surprising message coming from someone who dressed in a getup that reminded me of something out of a Salvador Dali painting.

His words about being practical have stuck with me during the past 30 years as I have spoken and written. When I read or listen to others, I have little patience for those who don't have a heavy dose of practicality. When I come across a person who skips over the practical aspects of explaining his or her ideas, I now realize two things:

1. This person doesn't know what in the heck he or she is talking about.

2. This person hasn't really done what he or she is blabbering on about—he or she has only had some phantom thoughts and somehow talked a publisher into putting those theories into book form.

Above all else, books that are worth printing—ones that are worth reading—are practical. They are books that can be put into action immediately, if not sooner!

According to the latest data I've read, out of the approximately 100,000 books published each year now, the average book will sell only about 2,500 copies. When it comes to Christian books, make that a bit over 1,000 copies. You may ask, "Why do so few copies sell?" There are, no doubt, many reasons for this, but at the top of the list is this fact: No one's life is being changed by the message of the average Christian book.

The book you hold in your hand, *Launch: Starting a New Church from Scratch*, by my friend Nelson Searcy bears no resemblance to the average Christian book. In the heart of every human on the planet Earth is an unspeakable desire to change the world around him or her—to depart one day having left a permanent mark that says, "I lived here once upon a time. I made a difference!" This desire is what causes people like Nelson and me and you to do crazy things such as leaving security, finances, opportunity and family behind to go to all sorts of strange places to plant churches. We desire to see people—lots of people—be eternally changed.

This is not only a super-practical book (I salivated as I read this work—Nelson delivers the goods with this), but it is also a book that will alter the path you are embarking on as a planter who is in midstream or pondering or planning a new church.

Currently, 80 percent of all church plants in the United States by the five-year mark will have been declared duds. This may be a cruel way to phrase it, but hey, it's the stark truth. Only 20 percent of all attempted church plants will fly, and of those 20 percent, what analysts call "success" is pitiful. Let's just say that if I were leading a church of that size and amount of momentum,

I would be looking for a tall bridge to jump off after five years of hard work.

Earth to reader: *It doesn't have to be that way!* It's been said by many over the years and bears repeating again: Leaders are readers! The fact that you've picked up this book tells me that you're well aware of this!

To lead successfully, whether you are focusing on leading a new church plant, a midsized church or a large "launching pad" church—whatever you have been called to—you must have multiple coaches in your life to attain success. Once you find outstanding coaches who will show you the way, do whatever it takes to get them into your life. Pay whatever price you have to pay—fly, walk, hitchhike, rollerblade (okay, you get the idea).

I have had 15 speaking coaches alone up to this point in my life. I have had 20 church-planting coaches. I suspect that I have invested well over $100,000 out of my own pocket in coaching of various sorts . . . I am not wealthy by any means—far from it. During a good part of that time, Janie, my wife, and I were living below the official poverty line. But we realized that in order to go forward and succeed, we had to receive coaching.

Well, today is your blessed day. While I suspect that for much of your life you have seldom had anything handed to you, that's all about to change! This book you hold in your hand is a super-inexpensive encyclopedia filled with amazing coaching insights. Simply put, this book is probably worth many thousands of dollars in coaching secrets that Nelson for some odd reason has chosen to give away for practically nothing. (You are wrong about authors—they get almost nothing for writing books. I've written 15 of them—they take an enormous amount of time to construct and you end up quitting at least twice along the way. Still, you finish them just because you love Jesus and love His Church and want to see it go forward in strength.)

One last point to ponder: Right now, there are a number of popular books circulating on the topic of church planting. In the case of the two currently hot books making the rounds right now, I was led to believe the authors had actually done what they wrote about. They implied they had done it. Boy, was I wrong! True, the authors had a tiny bit of experience in church planting, but certainly not enough to qualify them to write definitive books on the topic. It's sad that the Church is the one place where people hawk their theoretical message on unsuspecting people who assume the best about the authors.

Oprah was angry when she discovered that the author of *A Million Little Pieces* had made up the story, yet the Church world is exposed to the likes of this sort of misbehavior on a regular basis. If Oprah only knew . . . Yet I can absolutely assure you that Nelson Searcy is a "been there, done that" experienced leader, planter, pastor and speaker. There are not more than a dozen or two leaders in the United States who could accomplish what he has done in the little time he has had to do it. His story is simply astounding.

Steve Sjogren predicts . . . In a decade or two you might well be hearing people around you say to one another, "There's a new guy that's teaching me so much—I am so stoked! His name is Nelson Searcy. You just have to read his new book. It's on the *New York Times* bestsellers list, you know."

Nelson, bro, kudos for the amazing gift of *Launch*! I know the truth behind this book. You have opened your storehouse and given away the family farm on this one. Thank you for letting me write the foreword of your first book.

Steve Sjogren
Senior Leader
CoastlandTampa
Tampa, Florida
Kindness.com

Starting a church is a heroic activity. Thank you for preparing for this calling. In addition to church planters, this book is ideal for:

- The spouse and family of a church planter
- Those thinking of joining a church-planting team
- Those who think church planting might be in their future
- Those who are unsure of their calling and want to learn more about church planting
- Seminary students who wish to study church planting
- Senior pastors, mission pastors and church leaders of existing churches who want to sponsor a new church
- Mission leaders or volunteers who help start new churches
- Denominational leaders who encourage and support church planting
- Individuals who desire to support new churches
- Students of church growth
- Anyone looking for new ideas on how to better start churches

Although this book was written primarily as a guide for lead pastors, the information in this book can be easily adapted for anyone interested in church planting. Consider using it as a tool for group study with other pastors, church planters or church-planting teams.

So, you want to start a new church, but you have no idea where to begin. You know that *someone* out there knows the logistics of how to start a growing church—because they exist all over the country—but you don't know how to get your hands on the roadmap they used. Do the pastors of thriving church plants just know something you don't? How do you get started with the vision God has put in your heart? Where do you go for practical answers to your very real church-planting questions?

In 2001, when we first began to think seriously about starting our church (The Journey), there were a number of church-planting books and resources on the market. We set out to read them all. We were going to be nothing if not informed. Many of the books were helpful on specific points. Others painted in broad strokes, giving us clear boundaries as to what we should avoid or what key questions we should consider. Several taught church-planting systems that had worked at one time, perhaps in the 1960s or 1970s, but now seemed outdated and ineffective.

Rick Warren's classic textbook, *The Purpose Driven Church,* gave us a solid picture of what a mature, healthy church should look like. But even though Rick planted Saddleback Church with no money, no building and no members (which was exactly our situation), he didn't detail his earliest steps in that book. Rick has always said we needed a book specifically about purpose-driven church planting. We realize now that we were looking for a "how to" guide on church planting—an instruction manual of sorts that not only made sense theoretically but was also visibly working in a number of growing churches. Such a guide didn't exist.

Our desire to learn all we could about church planting led us to conversations with successful church planters across the country. What we found was not surprising: They had the same feelings as we did about current church-planting books. While all these books had their areas of usefulness, there was simply no comprehensive roadmap that showed how to build a new church from scratch. Many of the planters we interviewed had gone "off road" and were growing their churches with little guidance from current methods or resources. Because they often discovered their processes and principles through trial and error, most were excited to share their insights in an attempt to save other future church planters time and energy. Their generous points of view led to the discovery of an essential church-planting precept that is at the heart of this book: *When you discover a helpful principle about church planting, you must share it with others.*

Through innumerable conversations with diverse church planters and our own study of the New Testament church, we began to assemble this collection of contrarian church-planting wisdom:

- Your call to start a church is the most critical factor to the church's success.
- Don't be afraid to raise funds from other churches.
- Build your church from the outside in.
- Don't start with small groups or with a youth ministry.

- Use three to six months of monthly worship services to build up to weekly services.
- Don't try to gather the churched; stay focused on the unchurched.
- In the beginning, resist the temptation to do everything.
- You can *start* a church much faster than you think.
- You can *grow* a church much faster than you think.

These were mind-expanding ideas for us! They spurred the drawing of our own roadmap, which gave us the direction we had been searching for.

Since then, we have been trying to codify and relay these ideas in a way that church planters can easily access and apply. We have worked to develop teachable language surrounding the concepts, and we have even struggled to explain why some of these ideas, which go against the grain of traditional church-planting theory, are better, more practical and still every inch biblical. The book in your hands is the culmination of our efforts. It is the book we wish had been available when we started The Journey.

Our goal is not to provide you with theory but with a proven and strategic process to take your new church from scratch to success and significance. We are not giving you cliff notes or the easy way around—there is no easy way to start a church. The process outlined in the following pages will require *work*, *focus* and *discipline*. In fact, this process may actually be more difficult in the beginning than other church-planting systems. However, we believe that it will ultimately help you stabilize your church and allow you to reap a greater harvest more quickly.

As you begin to discover and digest these concepts, we suggest that you not think through them solely on your own. Just as iron sharpens iron, so conversation will help you dissect and apply these ideas. Study them with your spouse or with others on your church-planting team. Get together with other church planters and read this book together.

As you read, take notes in the margins and record your thoughts in a journal. Let the content spark ideas—whether or not you agree with us—about what God wants to do in and through you. If you encounter an idea that surprises you, don't reject it too quickly. Let the idea stir in your mind, and see what happens.

We will begin our discussion in chapter 1 by telling you our story and then expanding on the key ideas outlined above. In chapter 2, we will lead you into a serious examination of the call to start a church. From there, we will examine how to develop an initial strategy (chapter 3), how to raise funds (chapter 4) and how to structure your early staff (chapter 5). In chapters 6 and 7, we will look at how to design your first service and how to build your launch team. In chapter 8, we will explore evangelism, while in chapter 9 we will give you some basic insight into the early systems of your church. The final chapter will provide an in-depth discussion on how to apply what you've learned in a way that will move your new church to success and significance.

There is not one right way to start a church. While the Bible gives us theological guidelines for what a church should be, it is relatively silent on the logistics of getting there. This may be because the "how to" of church planting changes over time. Starting a church in the third century would have looked quite different from starting a church in our century, which is why the tenets of church planting have evolved so drastically. Based on our research, study, in-depth application and experience, we believe that *Launch* can serve as your "how to" reference guide for starting a biblical twenty-first-century church.

Since officially employing the *Launch* concepts to start The Journey, we have been privileged to share ideas through one-on-one conversations, through coaching networks and in seminars with hundreds of church planters across the country. We have seen the strategies that we'll detail for you at work in all types of churches—from those in small rural towns to those in large metropolitan cities, and all points in between. We have garnered unbelievable testimonials from every corner of the United States. This is no credit to us but to God working through the powerful strategic process we'll be studying together.

If you have been called to this endeavor by Him and are willing to follow the proven plan set forth in the pages ahead, you will be able to launch the thriving, new church that's written on your heart!

Foundation

According to Catholic Church teaching, there are seven deadly sins. Regretfully, we're not Catholic, so we have no idea what these sins are. However, we are church planters, and in church planting there are three deadly sins:

1. Lack of calling
2. Lack of strategy
3. Lack of funds

These three deadly sins will ensure that a church plant fails and fails fast (most likely in a very public way so that even the Moonies will point and laugh). Among evangelical Christians, the statistics for new church failure are overwhelming. It's the dirty little secret among church types. Jehovah's Witnesses have a better success rate than we do.

The first four chapters of this book deal with the inescapable issues of effectively starting a church from scratch. We've tried to make some of the boring stuff exciting and some of the hard stuff easier to understand. Forgive us if we sometimes get it the other way around. (We'll try to do better in our next book.) We'll also try not to offend any other religious groups from here on out.

10 Rejected First Sentences of *Launch*

1. A nun walks into a bar . . .
2. So, we were just thinking . . .
3. Have you slit the throat of a pig lately?
4. Hey, buddy, wanna plant a church?
5. It's not about you . . .
6. If we can start a church, you can too . . .
7. Call me Ishmael . . .
8. This is your church; this is your church on crack.
9. I can't believe they are actually letting us write this book [us].
10. We can't believe we are actually publishing this book [our publisher].

Starting the Journey . . . from Scratch

I (Nelson) know how it feels to want to start a church. Like you, I've been there, wrestling with the fear, the indescribable excitement and the sheer awe that God may have actually called me to such a task. In the year 2000, God began to stir this desire in my heart—the desire to start a church from scratch. Church planting, in general, was not a new idea for me, but the concept of me personally planting a church caught me off guard.

I had worked closely with and felt a deep affinity for many church planters. In the mid-1990s, I had been on a church planting team in Apex, North Carolina, while I pursued a graduate degree at Duke University. In the late 1990s, I worked extensively with church planters at Saddleback Church as the director of the Purpose Driven Community. Church planting was familiar territory. But I had never experienced a firsthand call to start a church—until the early fall of 2000.

It was a mild October afternoon in central Florida. My friend Jason and I had just wrapped up a Purpose Driven-sponsored event in the area and were headed to the airport. I was flying home to Southern California, and he was on his way back to North Carolina. To this day, the conversation that took place in that tiny rental car is branded on my mind . . .

We started out simply enough, talking about what God was up to in our lives. Jason, who was in the music business, told me that he and his band were in production on their next album. Hedging, I mentioned a few things to him that were keeping me busy, knowing that I needed to go further. After a minute of silent personal battle, I confessed to him that I thought God was calling me to start a church. He chuckled, "Nelson, every time we go somewhere you talk about starting a church—whether it's Florida or Seattle." I had to admit that he was right. I loved church planters and usually felt a strong connection with them regardless of what city we were in. But something else was going on here. "No," I said, "this time it's different. I think God may be calling me to start a church in New York City."

Whew, I had finally said it out loud! What a release. Now, someone else I trusted could help me discern God's leading. Jason and I committed to do two things based on what I was feeling: (1) pray about the decision over the next couple of months, and (2) not say a word to our wives—not something I would recommend, but it seemed right to us at the time. (By the way, remember Jason. You'll run into him again in a later chapter.)

The next few weeks were a whirlwind. God was working in my life and I knew it. I just wasn't sure what He was doing. I prayed, studied the Bible, read a few books on church planting and wrote furiously in my journal—all "in secret." I didn't say a word about starting a church to my wife, Kelley. It wasn't that I was afraid to tell her—we have a great marriage and communicate well—I just needed to make sure that this call was truly from God before I said anything about it. In our marriage and ministry together, we had already moved from the East Coast to the West Coast, and I knew enough not to propose moving back across the country until I knew that God was the one behind the idea.

The next month, on Thanksgiving afternoon, Kelley and I were at home watching the Macy's Thanksgiving Day Parade and waiting to meet some friends for dinner. She turned to me, out of the blue, and asked an unusual question: "Where do you think we will end up after Saddleback?" I still wasn't exactly sure there was an "after Saddleback" in our future. We both loved the church. We loved California. We had great jobs, not to mention a house that fit us perfectly. From all outward appearances, we were settled. But given the stirring that I couldn't shake about New York, I hesitantly turned the question back on her. "I . . . I'm not sure," I stammered, in a quiet voice. "Where do *you* think we'll end up?" The next words out of her mouth shook me to the core. She said, "I've been thinking a lot about New York City lately."

Don't you love it when God shows Himself in a powerful way? We had never talked about New York before. Never even considered the possibility of living there. Yet unbeknownst to us, God was diligently sending each of us the same message about the possibility of following Him there.

During the next hour or so before dinner, we tried to wrap our minds around what ministry in New York City might be like. I poured my heart out about the leading that I had been sensing. We could hardly get through dinner that night because we were so anxious to get back home and keep talking through the possibilities. After dinner, I showed Kelley parts of my journal and outlined some ideas on what starting a church might look like. We wrapped up our Thanksgiving Day with a commitment to pray about this calling for 50 days. (My pastor, Rick Warren, had not yet become popular for the "40 Day" spiritual journeys—perhaps we prayed for an extra 10 days!)

Approximately 50 days later, on Valentine's weekend 2001, Kelley and I flew to New York City. We landed on one of the coldest days in a decade. Not exactly the warm reception our Southern California temperaments were hoping for! Nonetheless, with two other couples, we prayer-walked around New York City, took in some great restaurants, and pondered whether or not God was actually calling us to be part of this one-of-a-kind city.

At the end of a spectacular (and confirming) weekend, we said yes to God's call to move across the country and start a brand-new church. That night, echoes of Sinatra lulled us to sleep: "I want to be a part of it, New York, New York." We were about to embark on the adventure of a lifetime. We were 100 percent sure we were making the right decision—until our plane landed at LAX the following day.

With the California sun came a host of doubts. *How could we possibly make this happen?* we wondered. *Are we crazy to even try? What about selling our house? Our cars? How could I leave my position at Saddleback Church? What about Kelley's job?* Throughout the onslaught, we kept reminding ourselves of God's calling and confirmations. Staying true to my strategic nature, I put together a "Move to NYC" plan that would have us settled on the East Coast in about 12 months. But, as He often does, God had another timeline.

In just five short months, God miraculously brought everything together. We sold our house, Kelley resigned from her job, we said goodbye to our friends at the church, and headed east. We arrived in New York City in late July 2001 on one of the hottest days in NYC history, as irony would have it. We had no money for our new church and nowhere to meet, and we were the only members. The realities of starting a church from scratch in a brand-new city were about to hit us between the eyes.

Keeping first things first, we started getting settled in our new Upper West Side apartment. I stuck with the project for about 24 hours before leaving Kelley with piles of unpacked boxes and hopping a plane to start raising funds for the new church. I couldn't wait. We had secured enough money to move across the country and I had a forthcoming salary from a job in the city (I worked bivocationally for the first two and a half years), but we didn't have a single dime for the church. Thus, my fundraising quest began. There's a rumor circulating among church planters that Texas churches have a lot of money they'd like to part with, so I lined up appointments with a dozen or so Texas churches and headed south. I struck out with 10 of the churches I met with, but two heard me out. Both of them eventually became key partners in our work.

Back in New York, in early September 2001, Kelley and I made a decision to get serious about meeting people in the city and preparing for our first service. When you decide to meet people, you will—and one of the first people that I met was Kerrick. He and his wife had moved to New York about the same time we had and were planning to start a church in the East Village. To make a long story short, we began working together in January 2002. (Don't worry, you'll get the long version a little later on.)

We don't have to remind you what happened on September 11, 2001. The attacks that rocked the nation occurred, more or less, on our doorstep. We could see the Twin Towers from the park in front of our apartment. I have never experienced such a strange and surreal time. For weeks after the attack, Manhattan felt more like a police state than an international city.

In the midst of the 9/11 tragedy, we were humbled as God continued to work and move our new church forward. Of course, working in the midst of such disaster was not the way we would have planned our first two months, but God had everything under control. Looking back, if we had stuck to my "Move to NYC" timeline, we would have still been in California on 9/11. God obviously had a reason for getting us to New York sooner than we had anticipated.

We had planned to conduct a series of monthly services from September 2001 to February 2002. That plan held firm after 9/11—with one exception. We had to move our first monthly service from Sunday, September 16, to Tuesday, September 18, because the hotel we were scheduled to meet in was locked down for five days after the attacks. In one of the many early miracles in our church, God sent us an unscheduled mission team from September 15 to September 18 to help us get the word out about our date change. This team literally gave out thousands of flyers on the street corners.

Feeling that I needed to speak to the devastation that we had just experienced as a city, I changed the title and focus of my first four messages to "Rebuilding My Life." Unfortunately, in the aftermath of the attack, New Yorkers seemed to become even more bitter toward God rather than more open. Much of our effort was met with fresh disdain from an already un-churched culture. Even so, God blessed our monthly services. For all of you number crunchers, here is what the attendance for our first six monthly services looked like:

The Journey Monthly Worship Service Attendance		
Month	Attendance	Notes
September '01	98	The post-9/11 service attracted a crowd, but only 13 real prospects.
October '01	35	Our second monthly service
November '01	42	Our third monthly service
December '01	55	Our fourth monthly service
January '02	63	Our fifth monthly service
February '02	67	Our final monthly service

On Sunday, March 31, 2002, we launched weekly services, with 110 people in attendance. The Journey was underway! I'd like to tell you that our growth trend was straight up for the rest of that year—but it wasn't. For example, the Sunday after Easter 2002, we only had 55 in attendance. That's when we learned firsthand that everyone who comes on Easter Sunday doesn't necessarily come back the following week! (For more on our specific growth numbers, see appendix A.)

As God was growing The Journey, He was also growing us. He was slowly preparing us for the long-term plans He had for our church—plans that we are still discovering each and every day. Since those first months, God has continued to give Kelley and me confirmation points along the way. We stand in disbelief and awe at all that He is doing through The Journey. When we think back to that Thanksgiving Day not so long ago, we can do nothing but praise Him for guiding us into His will. Of course, there have been tests and trials—there always will be. But seeing God work through the difficulties is part of what makes church planting so rewarding. We are humbled and immensely grateful that He called us to this work and that He has given us the opportunity to share what we have learned with you.

Launching Large

As we prepare to work through the strategy and principles that have helped us and other churches across the country launch successfully, we want to make sure you understand the overarching goal of what you are about to read. Here it is: *We want to help you start a church from scratch that will reach as many people as possible, as quickly as possible, and in the power of the Holy Spirit.* In other words, our goal is to provide you with everything you need to *launch large*. This underlying premise of launching large will guide all of our ensuing discussions.

Launching large is the ability of a new church to reach as many people as possible within the first six to eight months of existence. It's all about discovering and fulfilling potential. Of course, "large" is a relative term. Some might argue from our story above that we didn't launch large. However, given the church culture in New York City (or lack thereof), we actually did quite well. Launching large will look different for different church planters in different environments. Church is local, and launching large is as unique as the area to which God has called you. Areas that are warm to the gospel may lend themselves to a larger launch than completely unchurched areas. We have also seen the reverse hold true. Don't get too caught up in the numbers. Instead, focus on the potential of your area as you allow the concept to sink in.

At the same time, don't completely dismiss the numbers. Numbers are important in that they represent the people you have won to Christ as well as your impact on the community as a whole. Others have fought the battle of why numbers matter, so we won't argue that here. However, we do believe that every person in a community is a person who matters to God and who needs a spiritual home. God wants His family to be as large as possible. So, numbers do serve a purpose—not as a means to secure bragging rights, but as a tool for measuring the expansion of God's kingdom.

Ask yourself, *What would launching large look like in my area?* One way to determine a broad answer is to examine what God is already doing in and around your area. When we set out to start The Journey, we had a difficult time finding comparative churches because there had been virtually no successful church plants in Manhattan in the years just before our start. In the New York City culture of 2002, having 110 people at the launch of a new church was significant. Since then, other churches in the city have had a larger launch than we did. And, by the way, we are their biggest fans. We understand the truth that God wants to use many churches to reach our city—and yours. This is not a competition.

God's dream for your church is bigger than your dream. Our goal was to grow to 50 people within a year of launching. Again, God had other plans. Launching large is about *cooperating with God* to see His vision accomplished in an area. Don't underestimate that vision or your ability to tap into it. If God is calling you to this task, He's not trying to play Hide-and-Seek with His vision and goals. Take a moment and use your sanctified imagination to envision what launching large would look like for your new church.

Launching Quickly

Contrary to some schools of thought, healthy churches can also be launched quickly. We fully believe that a church can begin monthly services within two to three months of a lead pastor's having arrived in the field—we've seen it time and time again. From there, we recommend only three to six months of monthly services until the church launches weekly services. We have found that this combination of speed and momentum-building has worked well in new churches around the country.

Some have argued that you can start a new church even faster than we've outlined. Indeed, in many other countries, church-planting movements are being launched in under a week, or even in one day (see David Garrison's *Church Planting Movements*). Here in the States, however, we have found that a slightly longer "build to launch" time brings greater health over the long haul. Launching a church is a bit like birthing a baby—the gestation period matters. While a baby can survive a premature birth, he or she may face long-term health risks as a result. Resist the temptation to launch too soon.

On the other hand, others have argued that the process described here is too fast. (You can always find someone who will disagree!) Many propose a long gestation period for a new church, with small gatherings, core groups and high initial commitment on behalf of the early attendees. Some churches stay in this prelaunch stage for 12 to 18 months. The sad reality is that many of these churches never get off the launching pad.

There is always going to be a reason to postpone launching your church. Conditions will never be perfect. This slow approach to launching is detrimental to the overall church health and to everyone involved. Take the time needed to ensure that you are on a healthy track, but resist the temptation to wait too long to launch.

Launching from the Outside In

Launching large also includes launching from the outside in—which is perhaps the most radical of our "launching successfully" precepts. It is completely possible to launch a church in which the only Christians on the initial team are the staff (pastor, worship leaders and spouses). In building a church from the ground up, you don't have to wait until you can attract a set number of Christians from the area or until you can convince Christians from other areas to embrace your vision and relocate. God may bring those people your way, or He may not. They are not necessarily required. Throughout history, God has worked through believers and unbelievers alike. What makes you think your church will be any different?

Keeping the goal of launching large in front of you causes a shift in the early DNA of your church—you will have an outward focus from the get-go. Churches that launch large tend to stay focused on the unchurched, while churches that wait to launch often get distracted with insider concerns and the perceived need to "take care of the core." Keeping a new church outwardly focused from the beginning is much easier than trying to refocus an inwardly concerned church.

For Such a Time as This

Churches are launching large across the United States. In our work with church planters, we have seen many churches grow from 0 to more than 400 in 6 to 12 months using the strategy of launching large. In a Southern town with a population of 160,000 people, we worked with a church that grew from 0 to more than 250 during monthly services and then launched with more than 300 members. A church in an established major city in Florida (where many other church plants had failed), after accepting the idea of launching large, launched with more than 300 people and eventually grew to more than 400 members in 8 months. God is blessing the willingness of these church planters to let Him work without preconceived limitations.

We could tell you the stories of many others who have seen God move in similar ways. Often, churches that launch large are able to grow to several hundred people (or even to more than a thousand people) in a matter of just a few years. These churches then have the stability to start other churches with greater frequency. If that kind of harvest doesn't expand your vision of the potential that God wants to fulfill through your new church, then we don't know what will! What is impossible with man is possible with God.

Launching a new church that impacts the community positively, reaches the lost, grows rapidly, helps people mature in their faith, and then starts more new churches nearby and around the world is entirely possible—with God! When He calls you to start a new church, give all of the potential and possibilities over to Him and let Him lead your work. Then, and only then, will your church become a church of greater success and significance than you ever imagined!

Now to Him who is able to do exceedingly abundantly above all that we ask or think, according to the power that works in us, to Him be glory in the church by Christ Jesus to all generations, forever and ever. Amen.

Ephesians 3:20-21, *NKJV*

The Call to Start a Church

call·ing (n): a strong inner impulse toward a particular course of action, especially when accompanied by conviction of divine influence.

The majority of church starts fail within the first year. Why? Because the majority of church planters start churches without a clear calling from God. In order to plant a successful church, you have *to know that you know that you are undeniably called by God.* Period. There is no way around this truth. Thriving churches have always been—and will always be—built on a base of personal calling, not personal choice. So, before we go any further with discussing the details of launching a growing church, let's make sure that you are following God's lead.

Do you know for sure that God has called you to start a new church? We're not asking about your call to ministry, your call to pastor or your call to help people, but specifically about your call to start a church. The call to start a new church plant is not the same as the call to serve in an existing church or work in a ministry-related organization. You may be the greatest preacher this side of Billy Graham but still not be called to start a church.

In marriage counseling sessions that we conduct at The Journey, we often try to talk people out of getting married. Don't get us wrong, we are all for marriage—when it is ordained by God. But if God is not the one behind the idea, disaster will inevitably follow. We try to prevent that from happening. While calling off an engagement is painful (sometimes even traumatic), it's much easier than calling off a marriage. Preempting the self-made decision will prevent a lot of pain in the future. So it is with the calling to start a church. If we can talk you out of starting a church, it's going to hurt a little now, but it's going to save you, your family and the people around you a lot of hurt in the future. And if you truly *are* called by God to start a new church, we won't be able to talk you out of it.

Back to our question: Do you know for sure that God has called you to start a new church? Understanding some sources of improper calling may be helpful as you reflect on your answer. There are, of course, dozens of sources of improper calling, but these are the ones that we deal with most frequently:

- Unemployment
- Anger or resentment toward another pastor
- Disgruntled staff
- Easier than searching for an existing ministry position
- Parent or grandparent started a church
- Ego
- It's the "in" thing

If you think you may have allowed an improper reason, voice or emotion to lead you to the idea of starting a new church, back away now. Spend some more time with God. Seek the advice of someone in ministry who knows you and can help you gain some perspective. You don't want to move forward on a hunch or because you feel "pretty sure" that you should be planting a church. You have to be completely certain. The Lord clearly admonishes those who forge ahead without a calling:

> "Behold, I am against those who prophesy false dreams," says the LORD, "and tell them, and cause My people to err by their lies and by their recklessness. Yet I did not send them or command them; therefore they shall not profit this people at all," says the LORD (Jer. 23:32, *NKJV*).

On the other hand, when you know that you have been called by God, you can act boldly and decisively in any situation. While there will undoubtedly be moments and even periods of uncertainty, knowing that you are called to the work you are doing is what keeps you moving forward. The first year of a new church is not easy. Often, the assurance of your calling is the only thing you have to stand on. So making sure you've been called is absolutely crucial.

Let's look at some of the ways you can recognize a proper calling.

- *Prayer and Bible study*. God calls, and confirms His call, through prayer and Bible study. People who are called often feel that God confirms His calling every time they pray or read the Bible.

- *Surprise*. A surprise calling happens more often than you may think. Ministry may have never entered into your own plans for your life, when (surprise!) God intercepts your plans. It has been said, "When God is stirring in my life, everything familiar gets uncomfortable."[1] This surprise calling leads to a 180-degree turn in career and life focus.

- *Holy discontent.* While anger, resentment or discontent toward an existing church or pastor can be a source of improper calling, a proper calling will often carry with it a sense of *holy* discontent. This type of discontent is not focused on problems within a ministry but has a heart to improve the situation in a particular community. Holy discontent also comes when you have ignored God's calling in your life and you realize you will not find fulfillment until you surrender to His will to start a church.

- *Burden for the unchurched.* A proper call is always accompanied by the desire to reach the unchurched. If your goal is to change the Christians in your community, you are most assuredly not called to start a new church. However, if you have a strong passion to reach the un-churched, you may be hearing a call from God.

- *Godly counsel.* A proper call will be accompanied by confirmation from those around you. Seek out other leaders and (prayerfully) gauge their response to your call.

The Four Calls of a Church Planter

1. Your Call to Start a Church

" 'Before I formed you in the womb I knew you; before you were born I sanctified you; I ordained you a prophet to the nations. . . .

For you shall go to all to whom I send you, and whatever I command you, you shall speak. Do not be afraid of their faces, for I am with you to deliver you,' says the LORD" (Jer. 1:5,7-8, *NKJV*).

If you have been called to start a church, not only will the calling be undeniable, but you will also be able to trust that God will equip and empower you to do the work that He sets before you. When He is the one who has chosen you, it is because He knows that you can fulfill the calling, standing on His strength. The feelings of inadequacy with which you may struggle have no place in God's call.

Andy Stanley poses this challenge to potential leaders called by God: "You're afraid? So what. Everybody's afraid. Fear is the common ground of humanity. The question you must wrestle to the ground is, 'Will I allow my fear to bind me to mediocrity?' "[2] You must decide to walk into the adventure for which you feel God is calling you.

2. Your Call to Understand Your Spouse's Call

"This explains why a man leaves his father and mother and is joined to his wife, and the two are united into one. Since they are no longer two but one" (Mark 10:7-8).

If you are married, God will not call you without confirming the call in your spouse. Go slowly in this area and communicate clearly with your spouse about what God is doing in your heart. The call to start a new church is not easy on a marriage. Open, honest communication throughout the process is crucial.

As you begin the process of discernment, there are several things you need to understand about your spouse's call:

- *The timing of your call may not match the timing of your spouse's call.* If your call comes first, be patient and allow God to speak to your spouse in His own timing. Do not push. Just as God called you together in marriage, He'll call you together to start a church. If you move forward without your spouse, you are not only acting outside of God's will for your marriage but are also putting your future church in jeopardy. If your spouse's call comes before yours, realize that God may be using your spouse to gently (or not so gently) push you to move forward into God's plan.

- *The intensity of your call may not match the intensity of your spouse's call.* While sometimes both spouses receive an intense call to start a church together, it's not uncommon for one to receive the calling to fill a more supportive role. Don't assume that your spouse is not in sync with you because your levels of passion are not equal. The goal is to confirm mutual calling, not mutual intensity.

- *Make sure your spouse is fully heard, involved and committed.* If your spouse is not fully heard, involved and committed, do not move forward. This is your chance to be a good listener. Allow your spouse to share his or her thoughts with you. Do not make any decisions without listening to your spouse's point of view and involving him or her in the process. Before you step out on your calling, check, recheck and ask your spouse's friends to check that he or she is fully committed. Your call to your marriage always takes precedence over your call to start a church.

3. Your Call to a Place

"It was by faith that Abraham obeyed when God called him to leave home and go to another land that God would give him as his inheritance" (Heb. 11:8).

The call to a specific place can come as part of your original calling, or later. Generally, there is a clear correlation between who you are and the place God calls you to plant a church. While a few exceptional people are called to cross-cultural ministries, most of us are called to places that match our personality or life experiences. If you are called to start a church, right now God is specifically preparing you for that place. God is also specifically preparing that place for you.

While my wife, Lorie, and I (Kerrick) were in graduate school in Princeton, New Jersey, I worked at an inner-city church on the lower east side of Manhattan. During that time, God laid an undeniable passion on our hearts for the city of New York. After graduation, we were presented with various opportunities to move to other parts of the country for ministry work.

One time, we had an interview at a wonderful church in another part of the country. It was in the perfect location, offered a tremendous salary and had unlimited opportunities. Yet after the interview, Lorie and I looked at each other and, at the same time, said, "I can't get New York out of my mind." We knew that if we didn't follow what God was placing on our hearts, we would regret it for the rest of our lives. Two months later, we were in

Manhattan looking for an apartment in the East Village and preparing to start a church. The call was undeniable—together we were called to a specific place for a specific task.

If you already know where you are called to start a new church, think about how God has prepared you for that place. What life experiences have you had that will help you relate to the community? Can you see how God has been working in you already? If you're not yet sure where you should start your new church, these questions may help you clarify this part of your calling:

- *Has God called you to leave your current home?* Keep in mind that you may already be in the place to which you are called.

- *Are you passionate about a particular area of the country/ world?* Be careful not to confuse passion with personal preference! If you know that God has put a passion in you for a specific place, carefully examine the possibility that He could be calling you there.

- *Have you ever told God, "The last place in the world I would want to live is _____"?* That might be the exact place He is calling you to go. Remember Jonah?

If you are having a hard time pinpointing where God wants you to start your new church, take the time to do some research, talk with other church leaders, pray with your spouse, and study some examples from Scripture.

4. Your Call to a People

"When I saw this, I fell face downward on the ground. Then I heard a voice saying, 'Mortal man, stand up. I want to talk to you.' While the voice was speaking, God's spirit entered me and raised me to my feet, and I heard the voice continue, 'Mortal man, I am sending you to the people of Israel. They have rebelled and turned against me and are still rebels, just as their ancestors were'" (Ezek. 1:28–2:3, *GNB*).

The place you are called will be filled with many different types of people—young, old, rich, poor, single, families, and so on. In the next chapter, we will examine how to determine what demographic will be coming to your church. But, as a teaser, go ahead and begin thinking about the type of people God has called you to reach. One call that is universal among church planters is the call to reach those who do not have a relationship with Jesus. Whatever people group God calls you to serve, it will be made up of those who don't know Him.

New York is an international city. There is no lack of various ethnic or religious groups. The city is also economically diverse. The richest of the rich live right next to the poorest of the poor. As we prayed at The Journey about the people to whom God was calling us, we realized that there was no shortage of churches in New York whose ministries were focused on the poor and the disadvantaged. But there were virtually no churches that were equipped or had a passion for the city's young professionals.

Not only did God place a burning passion in our hearts for the young professionals of Manhattan, but He also helped us recognize that they were the people group to whom we would be best able to relate. God gave us a desire to reach the people we were most equipped to reach—based on our gifts and experiences. Being called specifically to reach young professionals does not mean that we ignore the other needs of our city. But our hearts breaks when we think about all of the young professionals living without God in this dog-eat-dog city.

When you think of a people group that you might be called to reach, does your heart break for them? If so, you may want to consider whether God is specifically calling you to reach that group for His kingdom.

Characteristics of a Call

Now that you understand proper and improper sources of calling and the four callings that you will encounter as a church planter, evaluate your calling in light of the biblical characteristics of a godly calling. These include the following:

- *Is your calling clear?* As Paul taught us, "God is not the author of confusion but of peace" (1 Cor. 14:33, *NKJV*).

- *Has your calling been confirmed by others?* When you are called to start a church, you will see confirmation from those around you.

- *Are you humbled by the call?* Humility is the proper result of a true calling. If the call is not bigger than you, it may be from you and not from God!

- *Have you acted on your call?* When God calls you, you are incapable of ignoring His voice. The Bible teaches us this principle in Matthew 4:19-20: " 'Come, follow me,' Jesus said, 'and I will make you fishers of men.' *At once they left their nets and followed him*" (*NIV*, emphasis added).

Taking into consideration all of the information you've just absorbed, revisit the question at hand: Do you know for certain that God has called you to start a new church? Nail it down. When exactly were you called? What were the circumstances surrounding your call? How did it match up with the sources of proper calling? Do you recognize the four specific calls in your calling? How? How does your call measure up to biblical characteristics? What is the emerging vision that God is giving you with this call?

As you think about your answers to these questions, we encourage you to begin a church-planting journal. In this journal, you'll record your thoughts about your calling, your vision for the future and, ultimately, your launch date. Today, start by documenting your calling. And write in ink—once you start moving forward, you'll want to come back to your confirmed calling over and over again.

Answering the Call

The call to ministry is truly the call to prepare. Here are some ways you can begin preparing for your call to start a new church.

Prepare to Lead

Starting a church will stretch your leadership ability in ways you've never imagined. Your skill level in this area will either help or hinder its development. You need to take the time to prepare yourself as a leader—even if you've never led before. God will supply what you need as you do your part to learn. Our prayer at The Journey has always been, "God, make us into the leaders we need to be to lead this church into the future." He always has and continues to do just that!

Other authors have covered the area of leadership in great detail (see appendix C for resource suggestions), but to get you thinking, here are some key areas you'll want to study:

- Entrepreneurship
- Innovation
- Staff management
- Delegation
- Marketing
- Organizational development
- Accounting

Prepare to Teach

The ability to teach and the ability to start a successful church go hand in hand. Even if you are naturally gifted in the area of teaching, you must continue to prepare and strengthen your skill. Get yourself ready to teach in a way that will benefit the people you are called to reach. For many of you, this may mean a departure from the teaching style you have become used to in other churches. Take the time to learn from those around the country who have effective teaching ministries.

Keep in mind that your teaching will be broader than what you do in a worship service. As a church starter, you will constantly be teaching. You will teach your vision to your early core group. You will teach your plan to potential funding partners. You will teach your strategy to the community. You will teach your systems to laity. You will teach yourself what it means to pastor a growing church. Strong churches are built by strong teachers.

Prepare to Depend on God

Just as your leadership and teaching ability will be stretched, so too will your faith. Starting a church from scratch is a faith venture. At every turn, God will be teaching you and taking you into deeper dependence on Him. Here's the key: As your dependence on God grows, so will your church.

In the end, God's calling always leads to adventure. Every time we respond to God's voice in our lives, we step beyond our comfort zone into the great unknown. It's then that we are living on faith. It's then that we must totally depend on God. It's then that we are on the adventure. As John Eldredge says, "The only way to live in this adventure—with all its danger and unpredictability and immensely high stakes—is an ongoing, intimate relationship with God. The control we so desperately crave is an illusion. Far better to give it up in exchange for God's offer of companionship."[3]

So get ready . . . responding to the call of God to start a church is nothing if not an all-out, faith-intensive adventure. Do you know for certain that God has called you to start a new church? If you can answer, *"Absolutely yes!"* then let the adventure begin!

Remain in me, and I will remain in you. For a branch
cannot produce fruit if it is severed from the vine,
and you cannot be fruitful apart from me.

JOHN 15:4

Notes
1. Ron Sylvia, *Starting High Definition Churches* (Ocala, FL: High Definition Resources, 2004).
2. Andy Stanley, *The Next Generation Leader: Five Essentials for Those Who Will Shape the Future* (Sisters, OR: Multnomah Publishers, Inc.), n.p.
3. John Eldredge, *Wild at Heart* (Nashville, TN: Thomas Nelson, Inc.), p. 214.

Developing a Strategy

Success begins with a specific plan to move you from where you are to where you want to be. In other words, success begins with *strategy*. Whether you're hoping to grow a business, start a family, get an education or plant a new church, you must have a strategy in place before you will ever succeed. Nothing happens haphazardly. We accomplish what we plan to accomplish. Just as God had a strategy for hanging the stars and Edison had a strategy for developing his light bulb, you will need a strategy for creating a church that will make a significant impact for God's kingdom.

Milkshakes and Modern Strategy

In 1954, Ray Kroc, a middle-aged milkshake-machine salesman heard about a small San Bernardino restaurant that was selling enough milkshakes to need eight machines. The little restaurant was a burger joint run by two brothers, Dick and Maurice McDonald. As any good milkshake-machine salesman would do, Kroc decided to convince the McDonald brothers that they needed to open more locations. (Of course, that would mean exponential milkshake-machine sales for Kroc.) He even volunteered to run the new locations for the aging pair. They agreed. A few years later, Kroc bought the brothers out, and modern franchising was born.

What we've come to know as McDonald's, or really as the franchising model in general, did not happen simply because Ray Kroc convinced the McDonald brothers to expand. Kroc built the McDonald's empire through the application of a very specific foundational strategy—one that still fuels McDonald's growth and development today. The power of franchising rests on devising a strategy that works and sticking to it.

Every time you step into McDonald's, you know exactly what to expect. You never have to wonder if they will surprise you with a different kind of cheese or a special sauce when you order a Big Mac. And have you ever noticed how you know exactly where the bathroom is before you even step inside?

Every McDonald's in the world adheres to the same strict strategy, which is why they have been so successful. McDonald's employees are required to train at "Hamburger University." They know how to fill your order without making you wait. They know the right questions to ask to make you happy and increase their company's profits. McDonald's also knows the right steps to take to reach the community.

Can you imagine if Ray Kroc had been even the least bit haphazard in his planning? What if he had bought out the McDonald brothers and then said, "You know, these hamburgers are okay, but I like roast beef. Let's throw that on the menu in a few locations. Oh, and don't worry about uniforms, just wear what looks best on you. Set sales goals? Nah, we'll just take things as they come." Obviously, your local McDonald's (and you *must* have a local McDonald's) would not exist.

Of course, you are not starting a business. Yet even though your goal will not be to serve hamburgers to the world, the principles of strategy development and application are just as essential to your success in church planting. Without a specific, well-thought-out strategic plan, it is impossible to launch a successful restaurant, high school, library, zoo in Kalamazoo . . . or church. As a church planter, you'll be glad to hear that Ray Kroc did not make up this idea of success through specific strategy. God did.

Biblical Blueprints

The Bible is full of strategy, both human and divine. In Genesis 1, God's plan for creation is immediately obvious. Each day, God created something specific, and each thing He created came in a logical progression. On day one, God created the heavens, the earth, and day and night. On day two, He created the atmosphere. And so on. He didn't create Adam until the earth could sustain man. Creation was strategic.

Later as we move to the books of Joshua, 1 and 2 Samuel, and 1 and 2 Kings, we find many examples of strategies that are human in origin, blessed by God and successful in their results. Nehemiah is a particularly powerful example of God ordaining and infusing one man's plans to bring Him glory (see Neh. 1–8). When Nehemiah learned that the walls around Jerusalem lay in ruins, he began to pray about the disgrace that the rubble brought the Hebrews. God gave Nehemiah the vision to rebuild the walls and then began showing him how to go about it. Nehemiah developed a clear strategy for rebuilding the walls of Jerusalem, complete with personnel, materials, a budget and a timeline. Under his God-breathed, strategic leadership, the walls that had been rubble for years were rebuilt in just 52 days. Notice that prayer was Nehemiah's first step. He then took hold of a God-given vision and created a specific plan to fulfill the Lord's purpose.

In the New Testament, Jesus often works through God-inspired strategy. In Mark 6:7-13, we find that Jesus has a strategy in sending out the disciples two by two. He tells them what they can expect and what to do if things don't go according to plan. In Matthew 28:18-20, Jesus lays out God's redemptive strategy for all of humankind—the Great Commission. In Acts 1:8, Jesus gives His final commands to His disciples. He clearly lays out a strategic plan to reach the world, instructing them to begin their evangelism process in Jerusalem, then move to Judea, Samaria and eventually to the ends of the earth. Now that's a church-starting strategy!

From Genesis through the New Testament, biblical strategies vary in length and in scope. Some have timelines of only a few days, such as God's work in Genesis 1. Others span months, such as Nehemiah's rebuilding of the Jerusalem walls. Still others have eternal timelines.

The greatest strategy of all is God's strategy for redeeming humankind. From the very beginning, God has had a plan to redeem His creation and restore the broken relationship between Himself and man. He has planned for us to spend eternity with Him. God's redemption strategy has been going on for ages, and it will continue until the return of Jesus Christ. If you have truly been called to start a church, you are becoming an integral part of the most significant strategy ever conceived. This is definitely not the time to wing it.

One of the most common mistakes that enthusiastic and well-meaning church starters make is to move to a new location and start trying to reach people without thinking through even a short-term strategy. Sometimes the culprit is not an unwillingness to plan ahead, but simply misplaced enthusiasm or the pressure to show immediate results. But as the old saying goes, "If you fail to plan, you are planning to fail." The Bible is clear on this:

> Don't begin until you count the cost. For who would begin construction of a building without first getting estimates and then checking to see if there is enough money to pay the bills? Otherwise, you might complete only the foundation before running out of funds. And then how everyone would laugh at you! They would say, "There's the person who started that building and ran out of money before it was finished!" Or what king would ever dream of going to war without first sitting down with his counselors and discussing whether his army of ten thousand is strong enough to defeat the twenty thousand soldiers who are marching against him? If he is not able, then while the enemy is still far away, he will send a delegation to discuss terms of peace (Luke 14:28-32).

Ray Kroc didn't build a single McDonald's without a strategy. An army doesn't march into war without first planning the details of obtaining a victory. God didn't establish the redemptive plan for the world without precise forethought. So why would you even consider starting a church (the only institution Jesus left behind and the only one that will last forever—see Matthew 16:18) without first developing a God-infused, specific, winning strategy?

Defining Strategy

A strategy is simply a logical plan that gets you from where you are to where God wants you to be. A well-planned strategy will help you be more faithful and more fruitful with what God has called you to do. The reality is that God has called you to something big. Starting a church from scratch is no small endeavor. But if God has truly given you a vision to reach His people, you can be assured that He has a specific intent for how He wants you to do it. His ways are bigger than man's. Take comfort in the fact that God has a specific plan to get your church to where it needs to be.

A practical strategy will save you time, energy and money. Just think about the children of Israel wandering around in the wilderness after having been freed from captivity in Egypt. Even though God had given them a vision of the Promised Land, they did not devise a logical plan to get there. As a matter of fact, because of Moses' disobedience, the Israelites roamed around in the wilderness for 40 years. Thankfully, if we will listen to God on this point of strategy, we won't have to wander through the desert of struggling ministry.

Here are just a few of the practical reasons to start planning your strategy now:

- *A strategy is a document of faith.* God rewards us according to our faith. Your strategy is a written statement of how much you are expecting from God!

- *A successful strategy provides structure.* Rick Warren says that you can structure your church for control or you can structure your church for growth, but you cannot have both. Your strategy will help you structure the right way from the outset. Structure is essential in the life of a leader.

- *Developing a strategy forces you to think on paper.* Thinking things through on paper leads to greater clarity. Planning cannot happen in the abstract. In Habakkuk 2:2, the Lord commands, "Write the vision down and make it plain on tablets, that he may run who reads it" (*NKJV*). Modern psychology supports the biblical notion that writing down plans and goals is a key ingredient to success.

- *A strategy provides focus.* Too often, a church planter's attention is scattered across a hundred different issues. Your strategy will help bring you back to what's essential.

- *A strategy forces research.* As we will reinforce later, research is important to your church plant. You will have to spend some time gathering applicable facts, stats and information to create a thriving new church in your area.

- *A strategy is good for your team.* Anyone you are hoping to lead needs to have a clear sense of where you're going before he or she will follow. A team can come to common ground and rally around a strong strategy.

- *A strategy saves you time.* For every minute you spend planning, you save an hour in implementation. If you will put in the work of developing a strategy, you will save hours and hours of heartache and hard labor down the road.

- *A strategy makes it easier to ask others for help.* People generally reject anything that is confusing to them. As you begin to build a launch team and look for funding, and so on, your strategy will provide clarification for your partners.

- *A lack of strategy will limit your church's growth.* Enough said.

Principles of Strategy Development

Before you can begin the actual work of strategizing for your new church, you first need to understand some of the foundational principles of strategy development. Here are five principles that, if taken to heart, will help you create a successful strategy.

1. Principle of Applied Effort

Experience tells us that there are two types of pain: the pain of front-end discipline and the pain of back-end regret. With the question of strategy development, you get to choose which pain you'd rather live with. (Obviously, we suggest the former!)

Developing a strategy is hard work. It's a long process that will test and stretch you. But it is absolutely essential to success: "Work hard and become a leader; be lazy and become a slave" (Prov. 12:24).

2. Principle of Relevant Application

While you may learn from others, you cannot copy someone else's strategy. In this book, we will offer you the help of broad reference strategies and lots of advice for starting your church, but you will need to carefully apply the information in a way that is relevant to your situation. God has a unique plan for every church planter.

3. Principle of Post-complexity Simplicity

In developing your strategy, it is going to get very complex before it gets any easier. There is an old saying among strategists that first you must get crazy, then get focused and then get done. So get ready to be a little crazy. Brainstorm like it's going out of style. Use lots of paper. Keep following the process, and everything will start becoming clear.

4. Principle of Direct Communication

As you think about developing your strategy, make it easy to understand. Jesus often spoke in simple language, and so should you. Use simple and direct language. Some people like to use complicated words as a way to cover up sloppy thinking (some people do this in their preaching, too!). Make your strategy easy enough for an eight-year-old to understand. Flowery language and "Christianese" will just get in the way.

5. Principle of Holy Reliance

Throughout this process of strategy development, make sure that you are wholly reliant on the Holy Spirit. God has the blueprint for your church already drawn out, so just ask Him to reveal it to you. He will give you all the wisdom you need if you are sensitive to what He is saying.

Before we turn our attention to the nitty-gritty details of a successful strategy, let me encourage you to stop reading and take a moment to pray. Ask God to open up your mind, your heart and your intellect to what He wants to share with you. Strategy development requires consistent prayer. So take a moment to commit this process, and all of your planning, to God.

Developing Your Start-Up Strategy

The rest of this chapter will focus on writing a start-up strategy for your new church. In order to have a successful strategy, you will first need to understand the eight key elements that comprise this strategy and see them in the context of an actual strategy document. To help you out, we've created an abbreviated example of what your initial strategy might look like (see Figure 1A), with element definitions built in. (Strategy worksheets are also available for download at www.church fromscratch.com.)

FIGURE 1A

Purpose, Mission and Vision Statement: The guiding statement that describes what God has called you to do (mission), how you will do it (purpose) and what it will ultimately look like (vision).

Core Values: The value filters through which you will fulfill your strategy.

Strategic Aim: The initial aim for which you are writing your strategy.

I. **Major Objective 1:** A title for the first key element you need to complete in order to fulfill your strategic aim. For example: *Preparation Stage*

    a. **Goal 1**—The first thing you need to accomplish toward Major Objective 1.
        i. **Task 1**—The first thing you need to accomplish toward Goal 1.
        ii. **Task 2** –The second thing you need to accomplish toward Goal 1.

    b. **Goal 2**—The second thing you need to accomplish toward Major Objective 1.
        i. **Task 1**
        ii. **Task 2**

II. **Major Objective 2:** The title of the second key element you need to complete in order to fulfill your strategic aim. For example: *Prelaunch*

    a. **Goal 1**—The first thing you need to accomplish toward Major Objective 2.
        i. **Task 1**—The first thing you need to accomplish toward Goal 1.
        ii. **Task 2**—The second thing you need to accomplish toward Goal 1.
        iii. **Task 3**—The third thing you need to accomplish toward Goal 1.

    b. **Goal 2**—The second thing you need to accomplish toward Major Objective 2.
        i. **Task 1**
        ii. **Task 2**
        iii. **Task 3** (and so on and so forth)

Eight Key Elements of a Start-Up Strategy

1. Purpose, Mission and Vision Statement

Much has been made about the differences among purpose, mission and vision statements. While these are valid discussions, we contend that most church planters spend far too much time concentrating on this issue when they should be focusing on other areas of their strategy. If your church succeeds, however you define it, no one is going to come back and fault you if your vision statement is slightly off.

Basically, a purpose, mission and vision statement provides guiding principles that describe what God has called you to do (mission), how you will do it (purpose) and what it will look like when you get it done (vision). Keep your statement simple. Be as precise as possible. (For some excellent resources on these statements, see appendix C.)

2. Core Values

Core values are the filter through which you fulfill your strategy. These are important, because your entire strategy will be created and implemented in such a way as to bring your core values to life. Generally, you will have no more than 12 core values. If you don't have any, or if you are unsure how to articulate them at this point, just use the great statements of Scripture as your guide. Your core values could simply be the Great Commission (see Matt. 28:19-20), the Great Commandments (see Matt. 22:37-40) and the Great Compassion (see Matt. 25:34-41).

3. Strategic Aim

Your strategic aim will serve as the beacon that guides the rest of your strategy. It is the initial purpose for which you are writing your strategy. Because you are writing a start-up strategy for a new church, your strategic aim will most likely be something along the lines of the following:

> *To effectively launch a new church in Great City, USA, on the second Sunday in September 20__, with 135 people in average weekly attendance during the month of October.*

Don't get paralysis of analysis here and feel that your strategic aim needs to be perfect. Just sketch out some initial thoughts so that you can move forward with the rest of your strategy. You can always edit later. (Note that in a sense, the rest of this book is designed to help you determine your exact strategic aim.)

4. Major Objectives

Major objectives are the key elements that you need to complete in order to accomplish your strategic aim. Everything else in your strategy will either rise or fall based on the clarity of these points.

In general, you will have four major objectives. In writing your major objectives, give each of the four a title, followed by no more than a three-sentence summary of what is to be accomplished by the objective. For a new church strategy, the four major objective titles will usually be:

I. Preparation
II. Prelaunch

III. Launch

IV. Postlaunch

You can use these titles or choose something more suited to your situation. Put some dedicated effort into laying out your major objectives in a clear and logical way, and you'll see that everything else begins to fall into place.

As an extremely simplified example of how the major objectives play out, let's look at a mathematical strategy. Say your strategic aim was to raise $100,000. Your Major Objective #1 might be to raise $25,000. Major Objective #2 would then be to raise an additional $25,000, and Major Objectives #3 and #4 would the same. When you accomplish all four of those major objectives, you would have fulfilled your strategic aim.

In getting started, sometimes it's helpful to visualize the major objectives laid out in a box format (see Figure 1B). This way, you can still see each objective separately, but taken together they illustrate the complete strategy.

FIGURE 1B

Major Objective #1: *Preparation*	Major Objective #2: *Prelaunch*
Major Objective #3: *Launch*	Major Objective #4: *Postlaunch*

Once you have completed your major objectives, you'll find that you have accomplished your strategic aim.

5. Goals

Underneath each major objective, you will want to list the goals that must be accomplished in order to achieve that major objective. These goals are tied directly to your major objectives and describe exactly what you will do to accomplish each objective. As a rule of thumb, limit yourself to no more than five goals for each major objective.

To go back to our simple mathematical example, if Major Objective #1 is to raise $25,000, then you might have five goals of raising $5,000. When each of these goals is accomplished, you will have fulfilled your Major Objective #1 of raising $25,000. Your goals add up to accomplish your major objectives, and your major objectives add up to accomplish your strategic aim. This is a step-by-step process. Once you have your goals in place, you are ready to develop the subset of those goals, namely, tasks.

6. Tasks

Tasks are clear actions that you will need to take in order to accomplish your goals. Your tasks are truly the heartbeat of your overall strategy, because they are where the real work happens.

You've probably heard the old riddle, "How do you eat an elephant? One bite at a time!" Well, in your strategy, tasks are your bites. You can have an unlimited number of tasks, so feel free to list absolutely everything you will need to do in order to accomplish each goal. Keep in mind, however, that it's common to leave tasks out of the external versions of your strategy. In other words, it's common to leave them out of the version of your strategy that you will be passing around to potential funding partners and other visionaries (see chapter 4).

As you accomplish your tasks, you will begin to accomplish your goals. Let's go back to the mathematical representation one last time: If your first goal under Major Objective #1 is to raise $5,000, you will need to accomplish certain tasks in order to raise that sum. For example, Task #1 might be to raise $1,000 through the sale of 500 widgets at $2 each. Task #2 might be to sell some property for a net income of $2,000. Task #3 might be to sell your brother's car for $2,000. So, when you successfully complete Task #1, #2 and #3, you will have accomplished your goal of raising $5,000.

As you can see, there is a logical flow within your strategy. Add up your tasks, and you have accomplished your goals. Add up your goals, and you have accomplished your major objectives. Add up your major objectives, and you have achieved your strategic aim. This follows a basic tenet of success: Every big accomplishment is achieved through a series of little accomplishments.

Eric Sevareid, a well-known war-time correspondent and author, told *Reader's Digest* that the best advice he ever received was the rule of the "next mile." Here's a portion of what he said:

During World War II, I and several others had to parachute from a crippled army transport plane into the mountainous jungle of the Burma-India border. It was several weeks before an armed relief expedition could reach us, and then we began a painful, plodding march "out" to civilized India. We were faced by a 140-mile trek, over mountains, in August heat and monsoon rains. In the first hour of the march, I rammed a boot nail deep into one foot; by evening I had bleeding blisters the size of a 50-cent piece on both feet. Could I hobble 140 miles? Could the others, some in worse shape than I, complete such a distance? We were convinced we could not. But we *could* hobble to that ridge. We *could* make the next friendly village for the night. And that, of course, was all we had to do . . .[1]

The rule of the next mile, which truly illustrates the step-by-step thought process behind strategy, is the most productive way to accomplish anything. Instead of initially focusing on and trying to reach the ultimate vision of creating a thriving church, you must take that vision, break it down and put your energy into completing the next goal, the next task and then the next one after that—until, eventually, you look up and find that your vision has come to pass!

When you have a draft of your strategic aim, major objectives, goals and tasks in place, you'll need to firm up your strategic statements with some SMART editing. Here's how it breaks down:

Figure 1C

S	*Specific*	All of the statements in your strategy need to be written in as precise language as possible. Avoid generalities.
M	*Measurable*	Make sure that you have some kind of gauge for measuring the accomplishment of each objective, goal and task.
A	*Attainable*	Break your statements into small enough bites that each one is realistically attainable. You can stretch, but don't overextend!
R	*Relevant*	Make each statement relative to the one that precedes it. For example, all tasks under Goal 1 should be directly relevant to Goal 1.
T	*Time Bound*	Put a projected completion date on every task, goal and major objective.

After you have edited every statement into SMART language, you will need to prioritize each element of your strategy. In our church-start example, we prioritized the major objectives by a timeline (Preparation, Prelaunch, Launch and Postlaunch). You may prioritize differently, but however you do it, the major objective that must be completed first should be listed first. Likewise, the goal that must be completed first to accomplish a major objective should be the first goal listed, and so forth.

As you begin the process of prioritizing, you may find it helpful to ask yourself, *Since I have limited time and limited money, what is the first major objective that would give me the most return on my investment? Which one would be the most important to accomplish? Which one is second, third, and so on?* The "80/20 Principle" states that 80 percent of your success will depend on 20 percent of your effort. So, what is the number one goal that, when accomplished, would deliver most of your major objective?

In the same way, make sure that you prioritize your tasks. This is logical, but it is a very important step that church starters often fail to take. As you begin to implement your strategy, you will find that you won't have the time or money to do everything you've planned out. By doing the hard work of prioritizing now, you will know what is most important to tackle first and what to leave undone should you later run out of time or money.

We want to encourage you to take these editing steps very seriously. Writing your strategy clearly is the key to communicating it well and successfully inviting others to get on board.

7. Budget

The final elements of a successful strategy are the budget and calendar. Many people make the mistake of creating a budget and a calendar before they think through their overall strategy. However, the simple reality is that if you have done everything we have described so far, your budget and calendar will be very easy to complete.

We will go into a detailed discussion of your budget in the next chapter, but your strategy is the perfect place to begin plotting out its development. Here's how you can get started: Beside each task in your strategy, list how much it will cost to accomplish that task. Once you have allocated a cost to each task of a certain goal, add those numbers together, and you'll know how much you need to budget in order to accomplish that goal. You now have a budget item. If you add up the cost for all of your goals, you will get the cost for each of your major objectives. The major objectives will become the primary categories for your budget.

You will certainly have to put more work and research into making sure that these numbers are on target, but this is the best way to begin an initial draft of your budget. If you commit to developing a detailed strategy, budgeting ultimately becomes much easier and more precise.

8. Calendar

Because your strategy is written in SMART language, every statement should have a date attached to it. These dates will become calendar entries on your start-up plan. When you have assigned each task, goal and objective a completion month and year (or, in some cases, even a completion day), list all of these dates in a spreadsheet (or simply write them out by hand).

Next, organize the items according to the calendar year. In putting together your initial calendar, you may find that the items are not evenly distributed. For example, if all of your tasks fall in the month of September, you're going to have a very busy month. So, you may want to consider shifting some of your tasks to August or October, or delegate carefully to your launch team during these crunch times (see chapter 7).

When you have your calendar in place, it will become the final pages of your strategy. You can then modify selections of this living document to use as a daily to-do list.

Spiritual Readiness

After years of doing crusades, the Billy Graham Association is able to predict, with astonishing accuracy, how many people will come forward for prayer on any given night. How? Because the number always correlates with how many volunteers they have lined up to receive those who respond! God will not send more people to Billy Graham than he is ready to receive. In the same way, He will not send more people to you than you are ready to receive.

So what can you do? The same thing Dr. Graham does. *Prepare* in a way that enables God to open the floodgates into your church. If you are truly ready, He will send people your way. If you do the work we've described in this chapter, you'll be able to build your new church on a strong base of God-breathed preparation. You'll know where you are, where you're going and how you are going to get there. You'll be standing in the rain with a huge bucket, ready to take in the deluge. However, if you don't think through your strategy, write it down and then implement it, you'll be like the man who stands in the rainstorm with a Dixie cup. You'll be completely unprepared to capture what God is pouring out. The choice is yours!

Commit your work to the LORD, and then your plans will succeed.

PROVERBS 16:3

Note

1. Eric Sevareid, "Bits and Pieces," *Reader's Digest*, February 1990, pp. 11-12.

Raising Funds

Zig Ziglar has said, "Money isn't everything, but it is right up there with oxygen." As church planters, we can relate to the sentiment! You may be sitting on go, ready to leave a secure job to set out on this entrepreneurial adventure. Or maybe you've already committed yourself full-time and now are realizing just how much money goes into starting a church. Wherever you are, the details of dollars and cents can be unnerving. But thinking through the issue of money is just as integral to the start of your new church as thinking through evangelism or strategy. One thing is for sure: No matter how strong your calling or how good your intentions, a new church cannot succeed without funding.

We've all heard the saying, "Ninety percent of success is showing up." In the area of funding for your church, you have to show up in a *big* way. One of the most common mistakes that church planters make is to plan for every other area of their church while pushing the money issues to the back burner. Too many even mask their unwillingness to deal with financial matters by putting all of the pressure on God: "He wanted me to start this church. He'll provide." Well, that is a completely true statement, but God does intend for you to do your part. You can rest assured, though, that if God is behind your church plant and you are moving forward in

His will, the money will be available to you. Funding follows faith.

> If God is for us, who can ever be against us? Since God did not spare even his own Son but gave him up for us all, won't God, who gave us Christ, also give us everything else? (Rom. 8:31-32).

So, the first step in funding your church plant is to know that you know that you know that you've been called to start a church. If God has ordained a venture, He will already have planned out every dollar that you need. All that you have to do is to tap into His unlimited resources and bring the money from where He's holding it to where it needs to be. So, how do you start this process? With a budget.

When I (Nelson) put together the first budget for The Journey in 2001, I realized that we would need to raise more than $100,000 just to *launch* the church. In Manhattan, everything costs twice as much as it does in other places, so dealing with the realities of budgeting was no easy task. Yet through this process, I learned the technical lessons that I have been privileged to share with church planters throughout the nation. In my experience with The Journey (and in working with hundreds of churches to help them put together their budgets), I have learned that budgeting is always a journey of faith. During the last few years, we have had to raise more than $200,000 in order to get the church to where it is today. And God has provided for us every step of the way.

Again, if God has called you—if you are in that place where God wants your church to be planted to make a significant difference for His kingdom—He will meet you around every corner.

God is in the budget as much as He is in any other detail that is essential to the expansion of His kingdom. So let's dive in and meet Him there. Time to get to work!

Creating a Budget

Creating a budget is the first technical issue in funding your church plant. Your budget will be the foundational document that tells you and your partners (those who are helping you start the church) what it's going to take to launch your church. As you begin preparing your document, the most important thing you can do to ensure success is to get cozy with the three *R*s of budgeting: research, research and research!

Do Your Research

An accurate budget must be built on a base of thorough research. You must do research on your community to find out what it will cost to get a church off the ground. You need to solidly answer questions such as:

- What will the cost of living in this community be?
- What will my salary be? How about salaries for additional staff?
- How much will it cost to rent space for the church to meet in?
- How much will it cost to operate a business in this city (office rent, phones, computer equipment, copy equipment, and so on)?

One time-tested way to get the information you need is to talk with other pastors in the community. Find out what their start-up costs were and what they are currently spending to maintain and operate the church. Other pastors can be a valuable resource for you on many levels.

Also, check with the local Chamber of Commerce. They often have prepackaged budget materials available for those who are starting a new business in the area. Even though you are not starting a business per se (church planting is not a business venture, it is a faith calling), you can and should draw from successful business principles when starting your church.

The worst mistake you can make is to start the budget process by viewing economic realities through a rose-colored lens. If you speculate too much or cut corners in this area, you'll end up paying dearly down the road. Remember, God never intended for you to go it alone. There are people and resources out there to help you prepare. Ask others for help. The wisdom of Proverbs rings true:

> Plans succeed through good counsel; don't go to war without the advice of others (20:18).

> Fools think they need no advice, but the wise listen to others (12:15).

Avoid Temptation

When you begin to put together your budget, you will face two competing temptations. First, there will be the temptation to think too small and try to survive on just the bare necessities. This nickel-and-diming ultimately leads to a scarcity of resources. If you estimate too small, you will have to do without—both in your church and in your personal finances. God receives no glory when you are scraping the bottom to do His work. So don't think too small.

Second, there is the temptation to think too large. You don't need top-of-the-line equipment and the nicest office in town right off the bat. Sure, we all want the best to represent God's kingdom, but it all has to be done in His timing. If you jump in beyond your means initially, you will end up being unrealistic about how much money you can raise and how long it will last. So be realistically conservative.

The wisest thing you can do is to seek God's counsel on how to find the balance here. Ask, "God, what is the right budget plan for us? What is the minimum I need to truly succeed for You? How can I invest the resources of the church wisely so that I maximize the resources You have entrusted to us?"

Undeniably, budgeting is a messy, hands-on endeavor. So to help you get started with the budgeting process for your church, we have put together a number of tools and resources that you can access at www.churchfromscratch.com.

Finding Funding

So, you have your initial budget in place. You've put in the hard work of pricing everything from space to staples and you've arrived at the number that is your bottom line. Don't get scared. Praise God in advance for His faithfulness, and then keep moving forward. Now that you know how much funding you are going to need, it's time to determine where that funding is going to come from. Here are a few well-tested funding sources.

Personal Savings

Your personal savings account is one possible source for helping fund your new church plant. Did that catch you off guard? Church planting is an all or nothing venture. You can't just partially commit. You have to fully commit, and often that means with your wallet. Almost every church planter has, at some point, had to dip into his or her savings in one form or another. It's a reality.

However, be sensitive to God's calling here. If you need to use your personal savings, make sure you're doing it in a thoughtful, Spirit-guided way. Some church planters completely exhaust their savings. Although that has been known to work in getting a church off the ground, it's not something we would advise. And it is definitely not something you should do impulsively or recklessly.

Bivocational Ministry

Another great way to fund your ministry is to work an additional job while you are planting your church. In other words, be a bivocational minister. If you decide on this option, you have to be careful to choose a second job that is best for your new church. Ideally, you want to find something that pays well and is flexible enough to let you dedicate to your church the time that it deserves.

For the first year and a half of our church plant in New York, both Kerrick and I were bivocational ministers. We worked other jobs for income but dedicated as much time as possible to the new church. Because my job was strong and secure, my wife and I made a decision that I should keep it for as long as needed. So, initially, Kelley was able to commit more time to the church than I was. My extra job provided some stability, guaranteed income and benefits such as insurance. God used that security to help take The Journey to the next level.

Remember, the key to having a bivocational job is for the job to be flexible enough for you to give substantial time to church planting. If you take this route, firmly establish an end date (as soon as possible) for when you plan to go full time with your church.

Your Spouse

In today's economy, your spouse may initially be a great source of funding. It can be a great blessing if you are in a position in which your spouse's salary is enough to cover the needs of your family, allowing you to focus entirely on starting the church. We know a number of church planters who have started this way, and it has been, by most accounts, quite successful.

Your Launch Team

Your initial launch team is a strong, logical source for helping to fund your new church. We will discuss the launch team in detail a little later. Just know that as you begin to reach people—and as those people start becoming part of your launch team—their tithes and offerings become a good source of funding. Never feel that you are taking advantage of your team members. If you blocked your team from tithing, you would be hurting them as much as yourself. And yes, it is perfectly acceptable to begin receiving an offering in your prelaunch services, as we will also discuss later.

Financial Partners

This is the big one. There are perhaps dozens of other ways that you can fund your church, but finding financial partners (even in addition to everything we just discussed) is the most important way. Let's explore this concept in more detail.

Asking the Right Questions to Find Potential Partners

Financial partners generally come in two forms: individual partners and church partners. As you begin to look for individuals or churches that will partner with you, there are several important questions you must consider.

Question #1: Who Do You Know?

First of all, ask yourself, *Who do I know?* Are there pastors with whom you have a relationship? Who is in your address book? What are the names of some individuals you could approach? Who has been supportive of you in the past? What churches are you connected to?

Don't just think about this in the abstract. Make a list. Write down the names of everyone you can think of who would be the least bit interested in supporting your new church. Perhaps most important, don't prejudge anyone. God is doing the work here. Don't limit Him by deciding in advance that someone you've considered putting on your list wouldn't be interested in helping. He's planning to use people you would have never imagined.

Question #2: Who Do the People You Know Know?

The second question you want to ask yourself is, *Who do the people that I know know?* This is obviously a logical extension of the first question, but it's often overlooked. For every person that you know, he or she knows three or four others who may be interested in supporting your church. If you already know some pastors, you're ahead of the game, as every pastor definitely has a strong network in place. As you begin to build out your list of people you know, leave room for the people they know.

We've all heard the Six Degrees of Separation theory, right? Sometime back, a study was done contending that everyone in the world is connected through no more than six degrees of separation. Some have argued that the world has become even smaller and that you may now only be three introductions away from any person you want to meet. While you may not be able to reach out to everyone in the world, every person you know and every pastor you know will have a network of people that they can tap in to. Once you convince individuals or pastors to get on board with you, it is easy for them to convince their friends or their colleagues to come along as well.

Question #3: Who Has a Heart for Your Area?

Third, ask yourself, *Who has a heart for the city or area where I'm planting my church?* If God has tapped you on the shoulder to be a church planter in a particular area, it's more than likely that He has already laid that area on someone else's heart, too.

As Kerrick and I began looking for partners to fund our work in New York City, this third question became the key issue. I knew that God had given me a heart for the City, but when I looked at the bottom line of our first budget, I had no idea how we would be able to afford to start a church. Then, as I started talking with some other pastors and individuals in the area, they began to tell me of people around the country who also had a heart for New York. When I contacted these people, I found that I did not have to do a sales pitch. I did not have to look for ways to weasel myself into their schedule. When I would mention that I was going to New York City, they immediately had an open door to receive me. Why? Because they already had a heart for the place where God was calling me.

As a matter of fact, our primary sponsoring church was a church that we did not know about at all. I had no connection with them, but God had already given the pastor a desire to be involved in New York City. Once I heard about this pastor, all I had to do was to share our plan and wait for God to confirm in his heart that The Journey was the right church to support in New York.

Remember, God already has the people in place. If you are seeking, He'll make sure you find them. We needed a lot of people to support what we were doing in New York because it's a big and expensive city, but if you are planting in a smaller area, you may need fewer partners. Remember, the size of your city and the number of unchurched people to reach will determine the number of people you'll find who have a heart for your area.

Question #4: Will God Show You What You Need to Do?

The fourth question is not directed to yourself but to your boss. Ask God, "Will You show me what I need to do?" God's resources are limitless; He knows more people than you could ever even dream of meeting. He will often times lead you right to a businessperson, pastor or individual you've never met before—just to give you the opportunity to form a relationship that can advance His kingdom. God has people who are more than willing to support your new church. You just have to be willing to ask Him to guide you and then go where He leads.

Question #5: What If the People You Ask Say No?

The last question is one that you are inevitably already asking—and one that you'll probably ask yourself a hundred times as you go through this process: "What if they say no? What do I do then?" There will be plenty of people who will be unwilling to support you, but never let it discourage you. When you fully understand that God is in control of this process, you will realize that you are simply in the business of finding the people He intends to bring alongside you. If someone tells you no, that person is not rejecting you or your church—he or she just isn't part of this plan. God will show you your partners. You just have to show a little faith in sowing the seed before you can reap the harvest.

Three Levels of Church Partnership

When it comes to handling a negative response, you must also remember that there are different ways a potential church partner can help you. If someone says, "Right now, we really can't fund you," don't take that as a completely closed door. Just because they can't support you financially doesn't mean they can't support you at all. Always go back to Question #2 and ask them who they know who might be interested in helping you. They might introduce you to your strongest partner. What you will also find is that churches will often agree to partner with you on one of three levels (assuming they don't reject you completely—and we've had plenty of straight-up rejections!): prayer, mission teams or financial support.

Level 1: Prayer

Some churches will just want to form a prayer partnership with you. Don't underestimate the importance of having a base of prayer partners. You need prayers as desperately as you need money. This could also eventually lead to greater support. Partners are usually more willing to come on board after they have associated with you and seen some success in your ministry. In the meantime, you can offer them a monthly prayer-update letter or an occasional phone call.

Level 2: Prayer Plus People

Others will want to pray for you and send mission teams to help you get started. To be perfectly honest, mission teams can sometimes be a double-edged sword. Although they can be a great blessing, they also run the risk of taking up too much of your time, forcing you to shift your focus to areas that you aren't ready to tackle. Be aware of the downside of too much mission team help so that you can work with them to maximize the blessing.

Level 3: Prayer Plus People Plus Paper

Ideally, what you are looking for is Level 3 partnerships—partners who will pray for you, send their teams and send the checks. It's always better to have fewer Level 3 partners than lots of Level 1 and Level 2 partners. If you have too many partners, you can fall into spending a great amount of time just trying to communicate with them. Meeting all of their expectations will be a constant weight. You'll find more success (and sanity!) with fewer higher-level partners.

Church Partners Versus Individual Partners

Your primary source of funding over the long haul will likely come from churches, not individuals. Partnering with churches has many advantages over partnering with individuals. For one thing, churches are more financially stable in the long term. If you recruit a large church to support you, it may be able to invest $10,000 to $15,000 for a number of years without any problem. However, individuals, even those who are financially successful and a strong source of support on the front end, will have personal rises and falls in their finances that may hinder them from supporting you year after year. They may also be unable to make a multiple-year commitment because their money is tied up in various investments. Churches are much more capable of making investments that span a number of years.

Churches can also offer more than just money. They can provide coaching, mentoring, staff assistance, procedural advice, training materials and a host of other resources for you. Often, they are not only able to raise large amounts of money, but they are also able to rally large numbers of people who can pray for you.

In terms of mentoring, we have found that it's critical to establish a relationship with the senior pastor at whatever church you are partnering with—no matter the level of their support. You may even want to consider working out an arrangement with the pastor that will allow you to learn from him—particularly if he started the church that is now supporting you. Although your first point of contact may be with a mission pastor, mission team or a prayer committee, don't overlook the importance of a senior pastor's commitment.

A word of caution on recruiting partners: Don't put all your eggs in one basket. Beware of having only one church partner or one individual who agrees to cover your costs. If you have only one church partner and that church experiences a setback, you'll find yourself in trouble. Even the most stable churches experience setbacks. Having a single financial partner is a recipe for disaster. In our experiences with at least a half-dozen churches that have used a single financial backer, all have turned out poorly. The best way to ensure that your new church is not dependent on one source is to diversify and recruit several partners. Diversification is good personal-finance advice—and it's good church-planting advice.

We hope that you will have success in finding individuals who will support you, but we also want to encourage you to be intentional in dealing with churches and securing them as your partners. Churches understand, from a perspective of experience, where you are and where you are trying to go. Overall, they are the best-equipped partners to support you—financially and otherwise—along the journey.

A person standing alone can be attacked and defeated, but two can stand back-to-back and conquer. Three are even better, for a triple-braided cord is not easily broken (Eccles. 4:12).

What Your Partners Want

Now that you are working on a potential list of partners, you need to know what those partners will want from you. Here are the 10 items that are most important to potential financial partners.

1. A Reasonable Strategy

Potential partners have to see that you have a reasonable strategy (refer back to chapter 3 for details on creating your strategy). Generally, partners focus on two items in a strategy: prior success and the launch date.

1. *Prior Success.* Potential partners will immediately ask, "Have you succeeded in other ventures that would demonstrate your ability to succeed here? Do you have what it takes to be a church planter?" All financial partners look to invest in success.

2. *A Launch Date.* Potential partners will also want to know that you have a plan for actually starting your church. Your launch date will speak volumes about your timing and how you will be spending your partners' money. (See chapters 6 and 7 for more on launching.)

2. A Reasonable Budget

Partners will want to see a reasonable budget (i.e., a budget that is conservative). They are really looking to make sure that you have done your research and that you are willing to stretch your funding and think innovatively in order to make this church happen. We have worked with some partners who really didn't care about the budget at all. At the same time, we have worked with others who have been overly nitpicky about the budget. If you do your homework and are prepared to back up every budget item, you'll be in good shape when recruiting partners.

3. A Plan for Self-Sufficiency

Potential partners will want to know that your relationship is not "till death do us part." They will need to know that you are not planning to rely on their partnership money forever and that your struggling church will eventually be able to walk on its own. When you have a solid plan for self-sufficiency, potential partners will be more willing to help you out at the beginning.

At The Journey, our goal was to become self-sufficient within three and a half years after our launch date. By "self-sufficient," we mean being able to meet budget needs solely from the tithes and offerings of our church attendees. Most churches operate on a self-sufficiency plan of three years. If your church is in an area in which the need is great enough, the city is large enough or there are some exceptional circumstances, you may be able to stretch this to five years.

Three to five years is about as far as most partnering churches will go in supporting you financially. Individuals, oftentimes, have an increased expectation of self-sufficiency. They want to see success within months or within the first year. You may have to work accordingly to justify your plan for self-sufficiency to them.

4. A Capable Leader

Potential partners are extremely interested in seeing that your venture has a capable leader. They want evidence of your past successes, but they also want to see that you are willing to learn from their wisdom and insights. It's essential for them to see you as a godly, capable leader who is growing and maturing. Partners must buy into the leaders of the new church before they are willing to invest.

A true leader longs to learn from other leaders. Countless senior pastors have told us that they resisted being involved with a church plant not because of a poor strategy or a poor budget but because they simply didn't have confidence in the leader. The church planter was too inexperienced, too inflexible or too impersonal.

5. A Clear Request for Support

Finding a partner is not the time to practice the art of subtlety. Potential partners want you to make a clear request for support. This is called the "big ask." God is putting you in front of people. All you have to do is ask for their support.

We have heard so many church planters lament about why a potential partner would not support their new church, only to discover that the person had not actually been asked for support. In our situation, early on in the process we would often meet with potential partners and become so excited over their enthusiasm for our new church plant that we would neglect coming to the point and directly asking them to financially invest in our venture. If you don't come out and ask people for their support, they won't invest. Never fail to make a clear request for support.

6. A Compelling Story

We live in narratives, not facts. People naturally love stories. So when you are talking to a potential partner, you have to be able to share why there is a need for your new church. Share with them your call to be a church planter and why your area deserves their support. In general, the more compelling story you have, the more support you will receive.

7. Other Partners

Partners will be looking for the security of other partners. It's a classic catch-22. They don't want to sign on until they see that someone else has signed on. It's a lot like the guy who is trying to get a job and the employer says, "You need experience," and the guy argues, "How do I get experience without getting the job?" Potential partners may think your strategy looks good, but often they won't be willing to support you without the backing of other partners. So how do you get the partners in the first place?

What you can do is start with the partners who you know are going to be the easiest to recruit. Find those friends, family members and churches with which you are most closely aligned and bring them on board first. They might not be your biggest financial partners, but it will demonstrate to potential partners that other people are on board. Nothing attracts new partners like other partners. Also, if you have a partner on board, you may want to ask that partner if he or she would assist you in recruiting other partners so that you are not sitting at the bargaining table alone.

8. Regular Communication

Potential partners need to know that you will communicate openly with them. They need you to acknowledge that communication is important. Reassure them that you will share your successes and failures and that you will give them regular updates on how their financial support is being used. In your initial discussion with partners, show them how you plan to communicate. This doesn't have to be a fancy, time-consuming newsletter. It can simply be an e-mail in which you report the basic stats on what God is doing in your church. (See chapter 9 for more on what to report, and visit www.churchfrom scratch.com for some sample reports.)

9. A Clear Opportunity for Success

Potential partners will want to see that there is a clear opportunity for success with your venture. We have already talked about how they will look at prior success when they view your strategy. Now, they will want to see that you have a clear plan in place to launch, grow and succeed.

There are many ways you can do this. You can share your calling and your qualifications to be a church planter. You can show potential partners how your area will be able to support this new church or how you will achieve your self-sufficiency plan. Before you ask for financial support, leave your partners feeling that your new church is a win-win establishment—a win for them and a win for the area where it will be started.

10. Results

Results speak volumes. Nothing distracts partners like laziness or inactivity. Show them the results of what you have already accomplished and the work you have already done in preparing for your new church. They will want to see that you are going to work your plan and that you are going to produce results. Church planting is probably the hardest, most frustrating and most fun work that you will ever do. It *does* take work, so show your partners that you are not afraid to put the hammer down.

Yes, you are dependent on God, and yes, you have this call, but if you are willing to give 110 percent of yourself to produce results, your passion will be contagious.

Holding a Partners Meeting

As soon as you have a partner in place, you are ready to set the date for your first annual partners meeting. The partners meeting will give you an opportunity to bring together all your key partners, potential partners and individual partners who have made a significant contribution to your new church. It's one of your most important undertakings in funding your church plant.

We suggest that you hold your first partners meeting before you launch and then continue to meet once a year for as long as you receive outside financial support. Invite the key pastors from your partner churches. The opportunity for them to connect with you and see what God is doing through their investment will keep the partnership healthy. These are not the easiest meetings to coordinate, so set the first meeting date well in advance and be sure to let each partner know that this will be an annual event throughout the course of your partnership.

Here are some practical steps to follow as you prepare to host an effective partners meeting. (See appendix B for a sample Partners Meeting Agenda.)

1. Host the Meeting at Your Location

Larger churches that you are in partnership with may offer to host the meeting for you, but don't accept. Instead, invite people to come and see what God is doing in your area. Show them the location where you meet. Show them your office. Introduce them to your staff. Let them meet your spouse. Take them to a local restaurant so that they can see the faces of the people that their support is going to reach. Show them the area around your church and cast the vision for your outreach. They need to see it with their own eyes.

2. Invite Current and Future Partners

Your current partners should come to the partners meeting so that they can see the young fruit of their investment. However, this meeting is not just for them. Invite others who are considering partnering with you. As we mentioned, nothing attracts partners like having other partners.

3. Invite Spouses

This is critical. Time and time again, we have seen God use a pastor's spouse from a partnering church to motivate that church to get more involved. The pastors' spouses often want to get the prayer ministry or women's ministry of their church more connected with you. On your end, there's no doubt that your spouse will value making a connection with the partners' spouses. In some of the partners meetings that we conducted in New York City, our wives found great encouragement as they forged relationships with the spouses of other pastors.

4. Make the Meeting Fun

Nothing happens until someone gets excited, so keep the meeting exciting! Make it fun. Go to a trendy restaurant. Do something in the park. If there is an area where you can spend an afternoon playing golf, go play golf. Be creative. Make your partners meeting a memorable experience.

If the fun requires a little expense, that's okay. Don't feel guilty about letting the partners pay their way. They will be happy to do it. They are supporting your church, and the last thing they want to do is to be an added expense to your budget. After all, if you spend a chunk of money keeping them entertained, they will begin to wonder if you are really using their money wisely. So, in the name of good fun and conservative budgeting, go Dutch.

5. Ask for the Big Commitment

If you forget to do this, you will have squandered an invaluable opportunity. While your meeting should be fun, informative and serve as a means to build relationships, that's not what it's ultimately about. Everything boils down to the business meeting where you will ask each church for their commitment, whether continued or new.

Yes, this needs to be an actual business meeting. Don't ask for your potential partners' commitment over dessert or on the golf course. Find a meeting room where you can all sit down to discuss the business of your church's success. During the business meeting, ask for your partners' thoughts on the day. Let them share what they have seen and what God is saying to them. Then share the short-term vision and goals for your church. Walk them through your budget, and make sure everyone has a copy to take with him or her.

You may want to consider asking the pastor of one of your partner churches to lead this meeting for you. If you choose this route, you will need to meet with this pastor ahead of time to go over the budget and to make sure that he or she is fully informed and capable of sharing your vision. You want someone who is willing to ask the other partners for the big commitment. If you can find someone who can handle the meeting well, let him or her do so. If not, step up to the plate, make your presentation, and request a commitment.

Next, invite each partner to voice his or her commitment in front of the group. To get this conversation started, you may have to prep some of your existing partners before the meeting to share what they have already committed to giving. Your future partners will then be encouraged to share as well. We're not talking about making a hard sell here or using any kind of coercive tactics—or locking the doors of the room until the partners commit $100,000. All you are doing is creating an atmosphere in which these issues can be discussed openly and honestly in a God-honoring way.

Remember, fundraising is an art, not a science. You can do everything that we have stated above and still not recruit the partners you need. Only God knows exactly how much you need and where it will come from. We often tell church planters that their church will cost them more than they think, but that God is bigger than they believe. Be encouraged—God is in control of your new church. He knows how much you need, and He will provide the right partners at the right time.

Journey of Faith

Once we put together our initial budget, recruited partners and worked through the technical issues discussed above, I (Nelson) found that God was doing something supernatural in my life. As I was reaching for funding, God was stretching my faith. As I was seeking deeper for these financial necessities, God was taking me deeper in my relationship with Him. Jesus said, "Wherever your treasure is, there your heart and thoughts will be also" (Matt. 6:21). I was looking for treasure—treasure to fund God's plan for this new church—and all the while God was growing my heart and drawing me closer to Him.

From those early days of starting the church when we wondered where we would get the $1,500 we needed for a sound system to today where we are thinking about how we'll get the quarter of a million dollars we need to take us to the next level, God has used every financial challenge to grow the faith of our entire staff and our church family. After all, when you see the needs rise and grow and then witness God meeting those ever-increasing needs at every turn, how can you but trust in Him even more deeply?

My personal journey with funding has really just been a backdrop to the greater story of God expanding my faith—and

I have a feeling He will do the same with you. Remember, funding follows faith. As you have faith in your new plant, God will bring about the funding. God does not operate on the scarcity principle. His resources are not limited. God operates on an abundance mentality, and He already has everything that your new church will need. Now, what He provides may not be as much as you were expecting—or it could be *more* than you imagined. Either way, it will be exactly what you need.

We love the quote, "Where God guides, God provides." We trust that God will provide everything you need to effectively start your church. But more than that, we pray that God will grow your faith exponentially during the journey.

Since we are his children, we will share his treasures—for everything God gives to his Son, Christ, is ours, too.

ROMANS 8:17

Formation

The most common question church planters ask us is, Why do some new churches succeed while other new churches do not? There are a number of good answers: (1) above-average leadership, (2) an anointing by God, (3) a good plan, (4) a careful reading of *Launch* by those guys from New York City.

And those are just the reasons listed under letter *A*. In addition, there's the possibility of first-mover advantage, focused strategy and funded adequately (to cover some of the *F* reasons).

All kidding aside, we believe there is an answer that accounts for at least 80 percent of the success of a new church. Here's our answer.

Think of the launch of a church as the birth of a child. What's the number one determinant of early health in a newborn child? A healthy birth. Every good parent prays for a healthy birth and then prepares with prenatal vitamins, careful medical attention and other measures. Likewise, every good church planter prays for a healthy launch.

An unhealthy launch may occur when a new church begins as the result of a church split, when a planter is disobedient in following God, or when there is a lack of funding or solid strategy. On a more subtle level, a church may not achieve a healthy launch because of poor staff decisions, a bad initial team (sometimes called a "core group," but we prefer the term "launch team"), or by being too hasty in trying to start weekly services.

The next three chapters focus on the most effective ways that we know to ensure the healthy launch of a church.

Top 10 Rejected Titles for *Launch*

Church Planting for Dummies
(our suggestion)

Church Planting by Dummies
(our publisher's suggestion)

Garfield's First Church-Planting Book

Planting Churches and Other Wild Flowers

Here a Church, There a Church, Everywhere a Church Church

Church Planting: When You Can't Make It in an Established Church

Starting a Church with Bags o' Cash

The Weekend Church Planter's Guide to Millions

Starting a Church with No Money Down

How to Start Big and Fall Fast in Church Planting
(Four Years or Less, Guaranteed!)

Building a Staff

John Maxwell says that the greatest leadership principle he has ever learned was that "those closest to the leader will determine the success level of that leader."[1] As you move toward building a staff for your new church, keep these words in mind. Finding the right teammates to help you on this journey is serious business. The people you bring on to your staff will either propel you down the road toward fulfilling the vision for your church or serve as speed bumps along the way.

No matter where you are in the process of starting your church, you probably only know one thing for sure when it comes to staffing: You need a staff. Right. Now what? When should you start hiring? What positions should you fill first? Where will you find the people? How will you pay them? How do you make sure you are hiring people who will increase your level of success?

Help Wanted

There are three critical staffing tenets that, when taken to heart, can help you wisely embark on this journey of staff building. Use these tenets as your underlying guide as you begin to consider staffing-related issues.

Tenet #1: Find First-Year Staff First

Sounds pretty simple, right? You would be amazed how many church planters start trying to fill positions with no long-term staffing plan in mind. They end up hiring for the wrong staff positions in the wrong order. Remember, there are *key* staff members that you must have on board during the first year of your new church:

- Lead pastor
- Worship leader
- Children's ministry leader

Because you are more than likely the lead pastor, that top-priority position is already taken care of, which means that the worship leader is going to be your most important first-year hire (later in this chapter, we'll go into more detail on finding a worship leader). The children's ministry leader is the next essential position, unless your target demographic does not generally have children. In that case, you only need two staff members during the first year.

This was the situation with The Journey. During our first year, we were primarily reaching single young professionals, artists and young couples without children. We made a strategic decision not to start a children's ministry, but rather to focus our energies elsewhere. In fact, we did not launch Journey Kidz until nearly two years after we launched our church. That was the best decision in our situation, and one that you might want to adopt if you are reaching a similar group of people. For most churches, however, establishing a strong children's ministry right from the start is essential for reaching families in the community.

During your first year, you do *not* need to hire a church secretary, a youth pastor or any other kind of specialized pastor (i.e., a discipleship pastor). Hiring for these positions too early is a common mistake that church planters make. Not only will you be in a better position to hire later, but you will also fill the position with a stronger person by having had time to effectively delegate these traditional tasks to volunteers and watch potential candidates perform.

When you cannot afford staff, you have no choice but to master the art of delegation. In the beginning, never pay anyone to do what you can get a volunteer to do. You will save money, see who your strong volunteers are and set a precedent for future volunteer involvement. This is especially true when it comes to hiring a secretary. Wait until your church has grown well beyond 100 people before you even consider hiring a secretary. Instead, as the lead pastor, you should develop systems for volunteers to do basic secretarial work.

Tenet #1 should serve as a guide to keep you from overstaffing early on, but it should not keep you from staffing for growth should your new church enter a period of rapid expansion. If you are growing like wildfire and need more staff than the traditional first-year hires, by all means, staff as you are led!

Tenet #2: Decide How You Will Raise Payroll Funds

What is your fundraising philosophy going to be? You'll need to make this important decision before you begin hiring. More than likely, you will not be in a position to pay salaries to your new hires, so you will need to work out an arrangement whereby they can help fund their position. You must decide how the money is going to be generated and distributed. When it comes to raising funds for staff, keep the following in mind:

- View raising funds as a short-term plan, effective only until the church can afford to pay a full salary.
- Never offer to raise funds for a new staff person. Let him or her be responsible.
- Never ask staff to raise 100 percent of their salary. The church should provide some percentage, even if it's a small amount.
- Raise both funds and prayer supporters.
- Don't ask staff to raise funds if you didn't raise funds yourself.

Raising funds for your salary or asking staff to raise funds in the early days of a new church start can be a win-win scenario for everyone involved. Your church will grow faster, and you will see the vital role that prayer partners play in the launch process. No doubt, God will use the fundraising arrangement to teach you to further depend on Him.

As we've mentioned, we both made the choice to be bivocational during the first two years of The Journey. This allowed us to pour all of the funds we raised into outreach. We used what staffing funds we had to hire our worship leader. God honors the wise management of His funds, so don't overlook the bivocational option.

No matter how you decide to raise the funds for salaries, you have to have a gauge for determining acceptable salaries. So, how much should you pay the lead pastor and staff? It's simple:

Pay as much as you can without limiting the future growth of the church. (The annual "Compensation Handbook for Church Staff," available at www.churchstaffing.com, is a resource that we have found extremely helpful in determining staff salaries.) Once you have the facts, you must make a prayerful decision regarding salary amounts.

To this day, the lead pastor sets the salary structure for The Journey. If you are uncomfortable making these decisions, especially when it comes to your own salary, talk with other pastors in your area to determine an appropriate range. We have seen church planters set their salaries too high and consequently hinder the growth of the church. We have also seen church planters' families suffer from a salary set too low. Do the necessary research, and then make an informed, prayerful decision.

Tenet #3: Don't Be Afraid of the "Big Ask"

Asking people to join you in your work can be one of the most intimidating tasks you'll face in starting your new church. Don't let it be! You should never be afraid to ask potential staff members to join you—even if it means a salary cut, a drastic position change or a significant new challenge for them. As a church starter, you must learn to ask people to join you in all areas of the church's life. God never intended for us to do this alone. He is in the process of building up the people who will ultimately form your team. But He's going to leave it up to you to invite them to come aboard. You can't let fear keep you from doing your part!

When you ask someone to join your staff, you are not asking that person to make a sacrifice. (If you have that mentality, you need to work to change it.) Instead, you are offering that person the opportunity of a lifetime. As you move ahead with each big ask, be sure that your proposition is clear, carefully presented and reflective of the vision that God has given you.

So, on to the first big ask: asking a worship leader to join you.

Finding Your Worship Leader

There are three things that every new church must have before it can be a real church: (1) a lead pastor, (2) a start date, and (3) a worship leader. Assuming you've taken care of the first two items, it's time to turn your attention to hiring a worship leader.

As you begin looking for your worship leader, don't feel as if you have to find that perfect person who can lead the full slate of future worship ministries. That's not the person you need to find at this point. Simply look for someone who can lead during your worship services. That's all. Now, this person may, in fact, turn out to be your ultimate worship pastor. Great! But to get started, your primary need is for a consistent worship leader. So, how do you find this consistent leader?

Think Idealistically

In an ideal world, if you could have your pick of any worship leader, who would you hire? Who do you already know? Who have you heard of that you'd like to meet?

Your dream candidates may be at the top of their ministry or at the beginning of their ministry. They may even not be in ministry yet—but you know that they have the skills and the heart to do the job. With no regard to their current position, who would you choose? Go after your top choice! Your pick may be number one on the Top 40 Billboard charts, but if God calls that person to be part of your new church, it will be a promotion. God is bigger than the Top 40!

When we approached our first worship leader for The Journey, it turned out to be Jason (who was in the car with Nelson when he first announced out loud that God was calling him to New York). At that time, he was the lead singer in a rock band. They had just released their second studio album. We went in knowing that if Jason said yes, he would be taking a salary cut, stepping out of a fast-track career and joining an uncertain venture. He would be taking a big risk. Yet after hearing the vision and spending time in prayer, Jason decided to leave his band and join us in New York City—even though he had to raise his own salary for the first year. A big decision no doubt, but one of eternal significance.

How easy it would have been for us to say, "Oh, he has it made. He's on his way to true success in the music business. He wouldn't want to leave that to work for a start-up church." But if we had thought like that, we would have been limiting God. God had a plan for Jason's life that included The Journey. If we had been afraid to extend the invitation, we would have done a disservice to God, to Jason and to ourselves. We knew that he was our first choice, and we went after him.

Even if your number one choice says no, God is going to honor the faith you show in asking. I (Nelson) recently received an e-mail from a church planter who exemplifies the big ask in action:

> I went for my dream [worship leader] this week. He is a leader who was at the Saddleback worship conference

last summer, singing at one of the tent stages around the campus. I called and pitched him on coming to our church. He turned me down, but now he's on my team looking for a worship leader to send our way. Maybe God will use the act of faith of asking to get me connected with the person God has for this ministry. I'm giving it all I've got.

Become a Headhunter

As you start the search process, set out on a mission to meet as many worship leaders as possible. Ask your friends who they know, attend worship conferences, ask your partner churches and do online searches. Become a worship leader headhunter and see who you can turn up. Be as aggressive as you can (without being obnoxious)!

Colleges and Bible schools are a great place to look. One church starter in Phoenix recently found an entire worship team at a local Bible school. Contact music professors or campus ministers and let them know what you are looking for in a leader. They may know the perfect person. If you do end up working with a worship leader who is a student, you may want to establish a trial period before hiring him or her on a permanent basis.

Still Looking . . .

What if you exhaust all of your resources and still can't find a worship leader? First of all, don't panic. God will bring you the right leader at the right time if you are truly putting in the effort. In the meantime, during your monthly services you can bring in a worship leader from an area church or even fly in someone you know from a different state. But once you move to weekly services, it's best to have someone on staff.

As we've mentioned, the key in these early days is a consistent presence. Perhaps you can get someone to lead worship on a short but consistent basis, maybe for two to six months. Or you could move ahead with creative options, such as prepackaged worship. You may also consider whether there is a layperson in your launch team that could lead well enough to carry you for a few months.

As a last resort, if you are unable to locate a worship leader, you may want to consider moving your launch date back one month. However, make sure that you are putting in the hard work to find a worship leader and are pursuing all of these options before you even think about changing your launch date. Finding the right worship leader may be incredibly easy for you, or it may turn into a quest you would never have predicted. Either way, once that person is in place, you will have filled the most important first-year staff position for your new church. Knowing that you have the right person on your team will make the pains you went through to get the person fade quickly away!

Using Staff from Partner Churches

Prior to your launch, when you are searching for staff members, don't overlook your partner churches. The churches that are offering you financial assistance will often loan their staff to you for specific projects or key events. If your partner relationship is strong, you may find that you already have a large staff available to you on a limited basis. Discuss this option with the contacts at your partner churches. Their willingness to step in may surprise you.

Early on at The Journey, we leaned heavily on one of our partner churches for help with graphic design. They had a full-time graphic designer who was willing to give one to two days a month to assist us with special projects. The designer's eagerness to help not only saved us money but also enabled us to stay several steps ahead of the curve in the area of graphic design. Partner churches have helped us with everything from advice on event and service planning to assistance in setting up accounting systems. You simply have to be willing to ask!

In addition to your partner churches, there are many resources available online to help with your staffing. Over the last several years, we have packaged much of what we've learned in ways that can be quickly accessed and used by church planters. Visit www.churchfromscratch.com to see how virtual assistance can help you get started.

The Power of Part-Time Staff

Part-time staff members are essential to the initial growth of your church. During the first year of your church and beyond, start looking around to see who is already putting in a significant number of volunteer and service hours. These committed individuals are often willing to increase their hours and become part-time staff for relatively little pay. At The Journey, we have found great success with three types of part-time staff.

1. True Part-Time Employees

Traditional part-time employees receive either half or a fourth of a full-time salary and are required to attend staff meetings. They have a set number of hours that they are expected to work and maintain office hours (if you have an office when they are hired— otherwise they work from home and are on call during certain times). As with all staff members, they have an approved job description and clear expectations. True part-time employees could include the worship leader, a secretary or office manager, a children's director, or even the lead pastor. Who you hire as a true part-time employee will depend on your particular situation.

2. $50-a-Week Staff

From the beginning, The Journey has used a kind of part-time staff that we call the "$50-a-week staff." While these staff members are paid significantly less than one-half or one-fourth of a full-time salary, they are still a vital part of our team. In reality, the weekly amount they receive may be more than $50 (sometimes it's $75 or as much as $200 per week). Employing the $50-a-week staff has been one of our most effective staffing strategies.

Here's how the idea was born: Early on, while we were still doing monthly services, we attracted a young college student to our church. The first Sunday he showed up, we only had about 15 people in attendance, so he was easy to spot. He didn't immediately stand up and say, "Hire me!" (Or we would have run quickly!) He simply kept coming back. Gradually, he started getting to the services earlier and earlier to help us setup, or he would stay late to help tear down. He was, in essence, our first committed volunteer. A few months later, we secured our first office space, and it wasn't long before this guy was stopping in to help fold programs, unpack from Sunday or do whatever else needed to be done.

After about four months of serving, this young guy had become quite valuable to us. We found ourselves depending on him every week, and he was always there. When he wasn't in class, he was serving at the church. We also saw that God was working in his life. He was growing in his faith by serving. So we decided to formalize his role. We offered him a $50 weekly stipend (you could hardly call that a salary) to keep doing what he was doing. He accepted, and we discovered the power of the $50-a-week staff person.

You might be asking, "Why pay him, when he was already so dependable for free?" First, we realized that we could no longer afford to not have him around. His value demanded accountability. Second, we wanted to reward his service in some small way. He was doing much more than $50 worth of work, but this arrangement gave us the opportunity to affirm him as a part of our team.

In our experience, no one has ever turned the $50-a-week proposition down, and the token salary secures quite a bit of additional commitment and accountability from an already dedicated volunteer. When a volunteer accepts the $50 per week stipend, we make him or her an official member of the staff and formalize a job description. Generally, we simply ask the person we are hiring to list everything he or she is already doing and then invite the new team member to add additional areas in which he or she would like to serve or suggest improvement to the new position description.

Once a regular volunteer has become so essential to the staff that his or her leaving would require you to hire a replacement, it's time to move that person to the $50-a-week level. If he or she later vacates the position, you will already have a job description in place, and it will be easier to replace that person. Likewise, if he or she starts performing poorly, you are in a position to remove that individual from staff. It's easier to remove a staff person with a formal job description than it is to remove a troublesome volunteer.

3. Interns

Interns are an extremely valuable source for staffing a young church. These are usually students who take one to two semesters off from college to serve with your church. (We often refer to our interns at The Journey as Summer or Semester Missionaries.)

Successful interns will have: (1) a set time that they are going to serve with you; (2) a clear position description; and (3) a big heart for your new church. Interns truly become part of your extended family, as you will generally help them find a place to live, serve as their career counselor, and basically do all that you can to help them have a great experience working in your church. As with all staffing decisions, careful preselection is the key to hiring an effective intern.

The big advantage to interns is that they pay their own way by raising their salary and living expenses. In our church, we ask our interns to raise at least half of the needed funds before their start date. You should also have a plan to help your interns grow in their faith and calling while they serve with you. This may include a weekly meeting time with you where you check in, read and discuss books together, or share what you both are learning about the church's ministry.

Many of our interns end up serving successfully in local church ministry. Some have even joined our staff after graduation. As a matter of fact, our very first summer missionary ended up moving back to New York City after her graduation and joined our full-time staff a year later. What started as a simple internship brought us one of our most valuable and committed staff members.

You'll be able to find interns from many different sources. Connect with your partner churches, contact your denomination leaders and talk with Christian organizations or campus ministers at colleges and graduate schools. (You may also find it helpful to visit our internship website at www.journeyleadership.com.)

Lessons from the Trenches

Staffing is an art, not a science. It's the area of leadership in church building that we have found to be more time consuming, heart wrenching and demanding of soul searching than any other. In the process, we've learned three difficult lessons that you will, hopefully, be able to benefit from.

Lesson 1: Hire Part-Time Before Full-Time

If you haven't noticed, we are committed to part-time staff. As a general rule, we prefer to hire a person at the part-time level before bringing him or her on full time. Hiring someone on a part-time basis first gives you a trial run. Both parties have the chance to assess whether the position is a good fit. You also have a chance to learn how to help your staff person be as successful as possible, which is truly your role as a supervisor.

The only staff member we let go during The Journey's first three years was someone we brought on staff to fill a full-time position. We probably violated a half-dozen other hiring rules with this person too, but if we had been able to see this guy in action on a part-time basis first, we probably could have prevented the heartache and fallout that resulted.

Lesson 2: Hire from Within

We almost always hire from within our church versus hiring someone from another church or outside our area. Obviously, you cannot hire your worship leader or children's ministry leader from within, as you don't have a church yet. However, three to six months after you launch, you will want to start looking to your own church members as you seek to fill staffing needs. The reasons for hiring from within have been discussed in detail in many other books, but in general the benefits include the following:

- The person you hire is a known commodity.
- He or she is already leading and has a track record.
- Hiring a church member means no moving expenses or acclimation time.
- He or she has seen your strategy and benefited from your ministry.
- He or she has an existing volunteer base to pull from (remember, you hire staff to lead teams, not to just do all the work themselves).

In addition, staff members who come from within have a longer tenure, as they are not looking for the next step in their ministry career. Most of our staff members have come from the business world, not the seminary world. While this has some disadvantages, we have found that those are far outweighed by the benefits of bringing on board people who are already active in our church.

How do you identify those people who would make good staff members? How do you help them work their way up? There is an overarching flow in moving people from volunteer positions to full-time staff. Ideally, here is how the process would work with a hypothetical church member, whom we'll call "Bob":

Step 1: Bob begins attending your church.

Step 2: Bob volunteers for a ministry.

Step 3: Bob does well as a volunteer and begins to lead other volunteers. (This would make Bob what we call a "high-capacity volunteer," a term borrowed from Bill Hybels.)

Step 4: Bob continues to do well as a High Capacity Volunteer, and you move him to a $50-a-week staff level.

Step 5: You hire Bob to a part-time or full-time staff position.

Most staffing mistakes come when you move a person like Bob straight from Step 1 to Step 5. The Journey's most effective staff people have progressed through each and every step.

In fact, one way to judge the future staffing potential of your church is to take the pulse on how many people you have in each step. Maybe it's time to hire some new staff!

Lesson 3: The Three Cs
When hiring a new staff person, make sure he or she possesses the three Cs:

1. *Character:* Is the potential staff member trustworthy? Does he or she have a track record of integrity?

2. *Chemistry:* Do you like the person? Is he or she easy to get along with? Does his or her attitude fit with you and the culture you want to establish?

3. *Competency:* Can the person do the job? Does he or she have the foundational skills necessary to learn to do the job?

Ask any organization or department leader, and he or she will tell you that most people are hired for competency and fired for lack of chemistry or character. Ensuring that all three Cs are covered before you hire will give you a head start and save you three *Ts* in the end—time, trouble and tears!

Clarity: The Holy Grail of Building a Staff

Every church will have its own unique path to growing a full staff. Whatever path you follow, there is one common denominator in all the staffing decisions you make: clarity.

You will need clarity on when to hire next. We have found that you will never have the money before you hire staff, so clarity is not necessarily linked to the financial reports. Rather, clarity comes from an assurance and confirmation that it's time to address the next area of your church that needs support and attention.

You will need clarity on how to structure your staff. A mentor once challenged us to always be thinking of our church as if it were twice its current size. Such future thinking usually brings a sense of clarity to the next staff hire.

Finally, you will need clarity on staff expectations. Whether a staff person is a $50-a-week staff member or the highest paid person on your team (in the early days, this may be the same person), always strive for clear, concise expectations. Develop a job description, hold regular staff meetings and set up evaluations to help bring clarity to this area.

Those closest to you truly will determine the level of your success. In no other area of the church is this truer than in the staff you build, lead and develop from scratch.

> Be strong and courageous! For you will lead these people.
>
> DEUTERONOMY 31:7

Note

1. John Maxwell, *Developing the Leaders Around You: How to Help Others Reach Their Full Potential* (Nashville, TN: Thomas Nelson Publishers), p. 203.

Top 10 Staffing Lessons from The Journey

1. You'll never have enough money up front to hire staff.

2. Hiring staff precedes growth, not vice versa.

3. Hire slow, fire fast. One bad apple spoils the bunch.

4. Hire from within whenever possible.

5. Hiring and firing is ultimately the responsibility of the lead pastor.

6. Hire part-time staff before full-time staff.

7. Never hire staff when you can find a volunteer.

8. The role of staff is to find additional volunteers.

9. Hold weekly staff meetings.

10. Clarity and accountability are the keys to an effective staff.

Planning Your First Service

Did you play high school sports? March in the band? When practice started each year, what was the one thing you were working toward? What goal did your coach keep in front of you? The first big game! There would be no point in training, game planning and teambuilding if your season had never been set to kick off. You knew when the game was scheduled, and everything you did was in preparation for that all-important night and the season to follow.

Your launch date is the kick-off point for your new church. It is the day you'll begin conducting services on an ongoing basis. Everything hinges on this date—funding, strategy, publicity, systems, teams . . . everything. A confirmed launch date is especially essential because it:

- Justifies your budget
- Builds excitement among your team
- Gives you a goal to keep you moving forward
- Creates a sense of urgency
- Sets your publicity plan
- Establishes your timeline
- Brings focus to your efforts

- Holds you accountable
- Shows partners and onlookers that you are serious

The launch date is the first big game after a long preseason of practice. It's the first milestone of your new church plant. So, it's time to schedule your launch date and start preparing.

Setting Your Launch Date

As you think about the launch date for your church, remember that your top goal is to *launch as publicly as possible, with as many people as possible.* You probably already have a date in mind. If not, think back to your original calling. When did you see yourself launching? Quickly write that date down—no second guessing, no mulling it over—just write it down now!

Unless the date you just wrote down is tomorrow, let's work with it. There are two things you are looking for in a start date: (1) a date on which you have the potential to reach as many people as possible, and (2) a date that precedes a period of time in which people, in general, are unlikely to be traveling out of town. With those guidelines in mind, here are three ideal start dates:

1. *Back-to-School Time:* When kids get ready to head back to school, families tend to settle down and stay put for a while. This is a great time to launch a church. Everyone has just returned from summer vacations and a new sense of routine is beckoning for the ensuing fall and winter. Back-to-school time is also one of two times during the year when people tend to reevaluate their lives and their goals. Also, because

most people move during the summer, this is a great time to attract new families (or new students, if you are in a college town).

2. *Post Christmas/New Year's Break:* By the time the carols have been sung and the ball has dropped, most people are ready to get back to the normal pace of life. Again, this is a time of year when people are reevaluating priorities and setting up new routines. Also, since many people have just broken their budgets with Christmas expenses, there are fewer travel and weekend entertainment plans in place. Christmas and New Year is also the time of year when depression is most common, so people are often more open to spiritual exploration. Early February is a great option for your church's launch date.

3. *Easter:* If an unchurched person is going to attend church at all, it will likely be on Easter Sunday. So this is a perfect time to give that person a new church to want to come back to. If Easter is early in the year, it can be the ideal time to start a church. However, if it falls later in the year, you'll have to weigh the benefits of an initial attendance boost with the drawbacks of those impending summer vacations.

Never launch a church on the Fourth of July, Thanksgiving Day, Christmas Day, New Year's Day, Super Bowl Sunday, the week schools let out or any day other than Sunday. The Journey launched on Easter Sunday, March 24, 2002. We planned toward that launch date from the beginning. Because this was a relatively early Easter and we were in the Northeast, we were able to build momentum and growth through April, May and most of June before summer vacation set in. Looking back, we would have preferred to launch in February. But once we decided on Easter, we were determined to stick with it.

Do everything you can to stick with your original launch date. You will always be tempted to wait until conditions are just a little bit better—until you have more people, a better meeting location, or one more partner. Conditions will never be perfect. We would love to tell you that everything about The Journey's launch was smooth sailing, but that's far from the truth! We had a million justifiable reasons to push our launch off until the fall. But we understood the significance of moving ahead on faith with the date God had led us to set. The best decision we made (maybe the only right decision we made during that period) was to stick with our launch date.

So, let's go back to the date you wrote down earlier. How much time do you have until then? If it's three to six months out and falls within one of the key launch periods outlined above, keep moving forward toward that date. If you are having major doubts (and we do mean *major*), keep reading, and let's see if we can find some clarity.

Monthly Services

You need steppingstones to get you from where you are to your launch date. We call these steppingstones "monthly services," though you may also hear them referred to as "preview services" or "sneak-preview services." Monthly services are real services that you begin holding three to six months prior to your launch date. They are the absolute best strategic precursor to your launch. At The Journey, in preparation for our Easter launch, we held six monthly services before beginning our weekly services.

Monthly services are more than worth the effort that goes into them. We have seen the majority of churches who skip this step start with smaller numbers and struggle longer. But remember, monthly services . . .

- Attract a launch team
- Build momentum
- Give you practice and allow you to improve your skills
- Give you a chance to grow
- Provide more time for follow-up
- Enable more efficient use of initial resources
- Lower your stress level
- Make your launch day less intimidating
- Build greater awareness of the church
- Build excitement within the church
- Help you stick to your launch date
- Allow you to test your meeting location
- Allow you to test a worship leader
- Build your database of future weekly attendees

Monthly services give you the invaluable opportunity to test-drive your systems, your staff and, to an extent, even your service style. At the same time, you are doing real ministry with the people in attendance. These services should mirror as closely as possible what your service will look like on the launch date. Don't bring in big name speakers or musicians. You and your worship leader should lead this service, just as you will lead future weekly services.

Keep in mind the following tips, which will help you make your monthly services as strong as possible:

Do	Don't
Teach a message series	Only talk about the future vision
Talk about your future weekly service	Tell them you are "practicing"
Receive an offering	Ask them to join
Put your best foot forward	Hesitate to evaluate and improve
Hold at least three monthly services	Do more than six preview services

A Common Question

Church planters often ask us, "How do I staff my first preview service?" In most cases, the first preview service is staffed entirely by the pastor, the worship leader and their spouses or older children. Because you will probably have very few people to recruit to help you with your first monthly service, you will have to find a way to do it all. At The Journey's first preview service, I (Nelson) took turns with our worship leader running the PowerPoint slides. I also served as the head greeter and usher. My wife and the worship leader's wife served as the preservice refreshment table managers and the postservice resource table workers.

You must be willing to take on any job that needs to be performed. Nothing is too remedial. This is your calling. There are, of course, ways to bring in outside help. After you do your first monthly service and you follow up with those who attended, you can ask them to serve next time around. There's also the possibility of scheduling mission teams to assist you during the other monthly services. But for that first time, adopt the heart of this poem by Edward Everett Hale:

> I am only one,
> But still I am one.
> I cannot do everything
> But still I can do something;
> And because I cannot do everything
> I will not refuse to do the something that I can do.[1]

With you, your worship leader and your families doing all the "somethings" that you can do, you can make the first monthly service smooth and successful.

Critical Mistake

The biggest mistake you can make at a monthly service is to *fail to collect basic contact information from those who attend your monthly preview services.* The people who attend your monthly services are the ones who have the highest potential of becoming your first regular attendees. Don't miss the opportunity for follow-up with those individuals God sends your way during this critical period of your church start.

As you begin to reach and follow up with people, keep these basic principles in mind:

1. *Follow up thoroughly.* Determine what method of collecting contact information on people is most effective (e-mail, letter, phone call, and so on), and then ask people to share their information. Be fanatical, but gracious, about collecting contact information. Do your best to make sure that no one falls through the cracks. Every person that you follow up with is a person God has entrusted to your care.

2. *Follow up quickly.* A fast follow-up is the best follow-up. You should start the follow-up process within a day or two of the event or service. Don't put it off. Enter the names into your database and start writing notes as soon as possible. Quick follow-up not only impresses the recipient, but we believe it honors God as well. You are showing the recipients that they matter to you—and showing God that you are thankful for those He has sent your way.

3. *Follow up personally.* A personal follow-up is the best follow-up. Now, this doesn't mean you have to call or personally visit people. As a matter of fact, in New York City, a phone call or personal visit is considered quite threatening. Instead, we write letters. Personal letters. Handwritten letters. We don't want anyone

to think they are just a name in a computer. They aren't! They are valuable individuals who deserve a personal follow-up.

At The Journey, we have even offered free books as an incentive for people to complete their communication cards and drop them in the offering. Once you have the contact information, you can follow up in nonthreatening ways and begin to build your launch team (see chapter 7).

Best Teaching Tip

Use a monthly teaching series. Remember, your monthly services are real services. A multiple-part series is a great way to keep people coming back for more. For example, The Journey's monthly services began just after the 9/11 attacks. People in the city were in desperate need of some truth to grasp on to. So we decided to do a three-month series entitled "Rebuilding My Life." The topic was relevant and helped attendees through a difficult time. Similarly, as you plan your monthly services, lay out a "felt needs" message series that consists of three to six parts *and* relates to your target audience and the time of year. Topics could include family, work, relationships, stress or success, to name a few.

Once you determine your series, promote the series name and individual message names on all of your publicity materials for the monthly services. Doing a series and announcing the message titles up front will not only attract people to your initial monthly service but will also give them a sense of what to expect and keep them coming back. For you, planning this monthly series will prepare you for the future reality of week-to-week message planning.

Nailing It Down

Now that you know the key times to start a church and understand all that goes into planning the monthly services, it's time to nail down your launch date. Hopefully, it will be the same date that you wrote down earlier in this chapter. Or maybe now you feel that you need to shift it slightly. Either way, open your calendar, get on your knees, and ask God to confirm your weekly start date. Do this now!

Once you have sought the Lord's guidance, thought through the information we've outlined above and have confirmed your launch date, don't ever change it. Don't let anyone or anything convince you to second-guess that date. We can guarantee you this: Temptations will come. The enemy will attack. The most well-intentioned plans will go awry. You'll have a hundred excuses to change that date, but *stick with it!* God has given you a vision, and now a date to launch that vision into being. Stay the course!

Now that you have your launch date set, you can begin building excitement for your launch, scheduling your preview services and finding a meeting location.

Location, Location, Location

Let your target demographic group be the strongest deciding factor in settling on a location. With your target group in mind, begin to make a list of every possible meeting location and the number of seats in each. The Journey's target group was 25- to 35-year-old professionals living in Manhattan, so this is the list we originally developed:

- Hotel ballrooms (various sizes)
- Movie theaters (various sizes)
- Comedy clubs (approximately 150 seats)
- Public-school auditoriums
- Performing-arts theaters
- Available church meeting spaces
- College auditoriums
- Corporate conference space

As you consider your potential locations, here are four guidelines for you to follow:

1. As much as possible, match your space to your target audience. (You wouldn't want the people of a rural, farming community meeting in a downtown art gallery.)
2. Make sure your space is easily accessible to your target audience. (You don't want downtown businesspeople traveling to the countryside—or anywhere else not easily accessed by public transportation.)
3. Make sure your space has a reasonable number of seats.
4. Don't sign a long-term lease.

You'll never find the *perfect* location, but don't let that hold you back. Instead, focus on finding the best possible location and then do everything you can to make it a great experience for those who attend. When The Journey launched, we held our morning service in a smoky comedy club and our evening service in a conference room that bore a striking resemblance to a funeral home. Not perfect. Early on, we also met in the basement of an old Ukrainian Orthodox Church (which one attendee described as having the feel of a drug den), a hotel ballroom, an off-Broadway theater and an elementary school auditorium. Make the best available choice, and then do all you can to make the space your own for your allotted time.

Don't discount the importance of continuity. Ideally, the space you find should be versatile enough to allow you to conduct your preview services and eventually your weekly services in the same location. This will provide an incredible sense of continuity for your attendees and put them at ease so that they will be more likely to come back. However, if space continuity is not realistic at this point, just make sure you have solid, effective communication with those who will be attending each month.

As you search for locations, keep a running list of places that may be too large for your monthly services or even your launch but might be perfect after six months of consistent growth. Always be on the lookout for the next space into which you plan to grow. Securing space often takes weeks (sometimes months), so it's never too early to begin building relationships with the people who manage "your next space."

Promoting Your Services

You now have set your monthly dates, a teaching series and your location. It's time to begin promoting your services! Welcome to the four *D*s of promotion: design, direct mail, display advertising and direct delivery.

Design

Create promotional materials that match your target group. If you are trying to reach senior adults in a retirement community, don't use 10-point type. If you are trying to reach urban singles, don't use bright colors and pictures of families playing on the beach. This may sound like no-brainer advice, but many church planters have made the mistake of mismatched promotion—including us!

Here's the best tip we can give on designing publicity: Find someone who matches your target group to design your promotion materials. Unless you are a marketing expert, don't even try to do it yourself. Your role should be to keep the promotion message on the right track and make sure that it matches your vision (see www.churchfromscratch.com for more resources on promotion design). With that in mind, here are a few design guidelines to have under your belt:

- Make the promotion match your city (use skylines, meadows, beach scenes—whatever characterizes your city best).
- Choose images that are attractive to your target audience.
- Be sure that text makes up less than 50 percent of your layout—period.
- Be clear that you are a church.
- State exactly what you want people to do ("Join us on [date]").
- Put your name, website, meeting times and location in a prominent place.
- Use full color. It's only a bit more expensive—but well worth it!

Once you have your promotion designed, you need to get it into the hands of prospective attendees. There are three primary sources of distribution:

1. Direct mail—low risk, low return
2. Display advertising/media—medium risk, medium return
3. Direct delivery—high risk, high return

Direct Mail

Direct mail is the most cost effective way to get your promotion out to a lot of people. It's low risk in that you can do it yourself for not a lot of money (the Postal Service will deliver your promotional materials for pennies). However, direct mail offers only a 1 percent return rate—which means that only 1 out of 100 people who receive your brochure will actually attend. Nonetheless, this is a great avenue.

There are two competing theories on using direct mail. The first is that you should send as many direct mail pieces to as many people as possible, all at one time. The second is that you achieve your best results when you send several direct mail pieces to a smaller number of people over a wider yet concentrated period of time. Your area, your target group and the size of your budget will determine your approach. For further guidance, talk to some direct mail groups that work with churches and direct mail businesses (mail houses) in your area.

One new slant on direct mail is distributing your direct mail pieces (fliers, postcards and so on) through distributors other than the postal service. Many church planters have found that for a reasonable fee, they are able to have their direct mail pieces inserted into local papers, which are then distributed by paper carriers. Others have used a similar process, often called "blow-ins," through regional or community magazines.

Display Advertising / Media

Display advertising is more expensive than direct mail, but it offers a higher return and reaches a more targeted population. It's medium risk in that you have less control over who receives the promotion, but also medium return in that you know more about the target audience. Newspaper advertisements and radio spots are the two best display advertising options. Other outlets include magazines, cable television, billboards, postcard rack displays and trade journals.

One of our most effective promotions at The Journey is through a trade journal for artists (one of our target groups). Each month via this display ad, we attract 5 to 10 people to our church. Another of our most effective advertising campaigns was a two-week targeted promotion on a popular radio station in our area. This station was the top secular station in our area and often listened to by our target group. One day during this promotion, our ad played during the station's morning show—The Howard Stern Show. While we raised a few eyebrows among the Christian community, the spot was extremely effective in attracting our target group. Too many church leaders make the mistake of advertising on Christian radio stations or in Christian publications. The unchurched people you will be trying to reach will not listen to Christian radio or read Christian publications.

To sum up, the top five display advertising media include the following:

1. Event-oriented newspapers (*Creative Loafing, What's Happening,* and so on)
2. The top radio morning shows (according to your target group)
3. Sports radio or the sports section of the newspaper
4. Local trade journals read by your target
5. Cable advertising on ESPN, CNN, FNC and others

Direct Delivery

Direct delivery is the highest-risk, highest-return option in advertising. Direct delivery includes everything from personal invites to servant evangelism, or any other type of face-to-face church promotion. It's high risk in that it requires person-to-person contact. If you are trying to make thousands of direct contacts, it will require the involvement of a lot of people. However, it's high return in that a personal invitation, delivered by a live person, is the most effective way of encouraging someone to attend your church. Here are three ways you can use direct delivery for maximum return:

1. *Invite everyone you meet!* You are the greatest evangelist for your new church. Always have a handful of postcards or other promotional materials to give to people you meet. With a smile on your face and the expectation of a positive encounter, talk to everyone and always have something about the church to put

into his or her hand. I know one church planter who refused to leave his house unless he was wearing a shirt that promoted his new church!

2. *Ask everyone you know—especially your launch team—to promote your church.* Load up your launch team with information about the church. Teach them how to effectively distribute printed information and talk about their new church. We have seen people become very creative in sharing. One storeowner put a stack of church postcards by the cash register. One office worker taped church postcards on the back of bathroom stalls in her office (we're not advocating using bathroom stalls and scotch tape—just sharing creative ways of promotion!).

3. *Join with mission teams or other outside people to help get the word out.* Servant evangelism is a great way to touch hundreds, or even thousands, of people with information about your new church. Simply having a mission team stand on a busy corner and hand out a pack of gum (servant) along with a postcard announcing your upcoming services (evangelism) creates incredible results. Schedule teams at strategic times and locations to maximize the effectiveness of your promotion. (See more on servant evangelism in chapter 8.)

We have been reaching people with all three of these methods since the beginning of The Journey's monthly services.

When it comes to getting the word out about your church, the bottleneck is not usually a money problem but an idea problem. When it comes to promoting your new church, be as creative as possible and enlist every person you can.

Planning Events

Planning events that will attract your focus population is key in effectively getting your church off the ground. In general, there are two types of events that you can use to reach people: single-sponsor events and multi-sponsor events.

Single-Sponsor Events

Single-sponsor events are those put on by you and you alone. Your church picks the location and is responsible for the agenda. Although single-sponsor events generally attract less of a crowd than a multi-sponsor event, they allow you to have complete control. You can share as much information about your new church as you like, and you'll have an easier time gathering contact information on everyone who attends.

Some examples of single-sponsor events include coffee house nights, picnics in the park, movie nights, holiday celebrations, play groups and comeback events. Play groups are one-time, fun events that are aimed at reaching new people in your community and building relationships within your church. At The Journey, we regularly scheduled these events to encourage people to have fun and meet new people—and, as a result, become more connected to the church and to God. We've since done Movie Night, Flag Football, Softball, Laser Tag, Pottery

Craft, Mom's Night Out, Bowling, Games in the Park, and on and on and on.

Because play groups are not ongoing, they require very little commitment, are open to everyone, and are perfect for inviting friends or first-time guests. The key is that they must be attractive to people and allow for personal interaction. We also always pray at our play groups and use them as opportunities to invite people to get plugged in further—whether it be to invite them to a Sunday service or encourage them to join a small group.

Comeback events are those events you schedule to invite those who attended a service to come back for a nonthreatening, fellowship-based event. For example, let's say your monthly services are on the second Sunday of every month. Perhaps you could plan to hold a comeback event on the fourth Saturday or Sunday of each month. At The Journey, we did several movie nights between our monthly services. Other churches have planned coffee nights, barbeques, Saturday picnics in the park and even gatherings at the pastor's home. Be creative. Just keep in mind that these should be low-risk, high-relationship events.

Holiday events also offer a unique opportunity for a new church to make its presence felt. If there is not currently a holiday-themed, community-wide event in your area, you will have the chance to own such an event. For example, let's say you are starting your church in a community that doesn't already have an annual Easter Egg Hunt. You can sponsor the first one. If you do it well, you'll be the Easter Egg Hunt organizers for a long time to come. Many times, we have seen a new church attract a thousand people or more to a first-time community-wide Easter Egg Hunt. It's a great way to introduce yourself to the community and to keep reintroducing your church year after year. The same idea could apply to many other holidays. Be creative!

Multi-Sponsor Events

A multi-sponsor event is usually a standing community event that you can choose to take part in. For example, if you know of a community music festival being planned in your downtown area, you could rent an exhibitor booth and offer a service that would attract your focus population. You could offer:

- Free bottles of water
- Free face painting for kids
- A rest station where people can sit and cool down
- Prayer stations

At the same time, your launch team could serve as general volunteers at the multi-sponsor event as a way to meet people in the area. While it can be more difficult to directly talk about your church at multi-sponsor events, the sheer number of people you can come into contact with makes participating in such events worthwhile.

Game Time

Your launch day should be promoted during each of your monthly services, on your website, and in every conversation with people that you have, so you need to make sure you have clarity on how you are positioning it. What will you call this big day? You could simply call it your Launch Day, Grand Opening, or Kick-Off. Decide what works best for you and promote it to the max. If you promote your church tenaciously and enthusiastically, people in your emerging church and in the community will be more likely to attend this service than any other.

Assuming that your monthly services have gone well and that you have used the time to work out any kinks, the launch service should go smoothly. However, you should always keep these things in mind as you prepare for the big day:

- *Have your people commit to inviting their friends.* Ask those who have attended your monthly services to commit to bringing at least one friend or family member to the launch. One pastor, who launched large, challenged each of his monthly attendees to bring 10 people. He even had every person give him the names of those 10 people—a great idea!

- *Launch with a new teaching series that hits a high felt-need of your target.* By beginning a series on your launch date, you are increasing your chances that people will attend initially and continue coming back.

- *Promote the next week and challenge people to come back.* On your launch day, challenge people to attend the entire series. Build anticipation for the upcoming weeks.

- *Challenge new people to tell their friends about the church.* There's a lot of excitement around your first weekly service. Use it to your advantage. Remind people to bring a friend with them the following week, and give them printed materials they can share with others.

• *Don't use an outside band/teacher for the launch service.* This would only set up false expectations. As much as possible, your launch service should reflect what your church will look like every week. Resist the temptation to go over the top with your launch service. It will hurt you in the long run.

• *Ask those who have attended the monthly services to serve at the launch.* Your monthly services will provide you with a pool of prospective volunteers that you can ask to serve on launch day. Personally invite people to serve, create a positive atmosphere, and overstaff in order to involve as many people as possible. This is a great time to learn and start implementing one of the top skills of church growth: delegate, delegate, delegate. Don't worry about perfection as much as involvement.

• *Collect contact information on everyone who attends.* Don't forget the basics. Provide a communication card to collect information on everyone who attends. No matter what happens at the launch, if you have follow-up information, you are off and running.

• *Count how many attend, and distinguish between in-town and out-of-town attendees.* Count how many real attendees you have at your first service. You will be tempted to count every warm body present. Resist this temptation! Instead, be honest about how many people attended who have the potential of truly becoming a part of the church.

- *Serve refreshments.* Go all out here. Get the best. Food is a powerful, often overlooked tool. The refreshments you serve can go a long way toward positioning your church as a fun and welcoming place. A plentiful refreshment table is a great way to show people you care about them. Here are a few refreshment-related tips:

Do	Don't
Serve fresh Krispy Kremes	Serve day-old, store-bought anything
Offer sweet, salty and healthy foods	Offer small portions
Offer name-brand drinks	Offer Sam's Choice
Offer water	Have a sign pointing to the fountain
Put smiling people out to serve	Let your team eat all the food
Provide food for your set-up teams	Tell anyone he or she can only have one of anything
Provide more than enough food	Comment when people take seconds or thirds

- *Set up your room so that it feels full.* An entire book could be written on how to set up a room (many have been—check out *Event Planning for Dummies*). Set up your room for the number of people you realistically think will attend and have plenty of extra chairs available. Also make sure that there is enough room between the aisles.

- *Keep the service to one hour*. That's 60 minutes. Period.

- *Receive an offering*. Receiving an offering is not offensive to those who attend your first service, especially if you handle it well and preplan what you are going to say. Perhaps something along these lines: "Giving an offering is an important part of worship. We want to invite you to participate by dropping your offering into the buckets as they are passed. However, if this is your first time with us, please do not feel obligated to give. Thank you for making the ministry of this church possible."

- *Meet as many people as possible at your launch*. Make sure you are visible and accessible during the 10 minutes before and 10 minutes after the service. Don't be in the back praying with the worship team before the service or immediately start tearing down the equipment after the service. First-time guests will arrive late and leave immediately. Be available to them. (For more ideas on how to treat first-time guest, see the "Assimilation Seminar" referenced in appendix C.)

- *Be ready for the Sunday after your launch*. Once you launch, there's no turning back. Many church planters are surprised that as soon as the launch is over, they have to start preparing for the following Sunday. Remember, Sunday comes every seven days. The big one may be behind you, but you get to do it all over again next week!

Former NFL quarterback Roger Staubach once said, "Spectacular achievements come from unspectacular preparation." This rings true in every person's life but perhaps most profoundly for the church planter on the cusp of a launch. Think clearly and carefully about your first service. Talk to others who have launched churches and invite their feedback on your plan. Remember, this is it. It's the first game of the biggest season of your life. Make sure you are ready. A successful launch can help you break early growth barriers and give you the momentum you need for incredible expansion!

> "For I know the plans I have for you," says the LORD.
> "They are plans for good and not for disaster,
> to give you a future and a hope."
>
> JEREMIAH 29:11

Note

1. Edward Everett Hale, "Affirmation No. 457," *Singing the Living Tradition* (Boston, MA: Unitarian Universalist Association, Beacon Press, 1993), n.p.

Gathering a
Launch Team

The old cliché is true: "You plus God equals a majority." And the Scriptures are clear: "You can do all things through Christ who strengthens you" (see Phil. 4:13). Citing these two realities as foundation, many church planters are tempted to think that they don't need a fully formed team to help them launch. They think they can do it all. Generally, this false sense of confidence stems not from solid faith in the gifts God has endowed to them, but instead is a cover for their fear: fear of rejection . . . fear of investing in the wrong people . . . fear of delegating responsibility . . . fear of not knowing how to gather an effective launch team.

We can relate. When we arrived in New York City to start The Journey, we did not have a launch team. We didn't even know anyone in the New York area. An intimidating position to be in, yes, but also one that carried many advantages. In our opinion, having to build a launch team from scratch is ultimately the best-case scenario for your launch. But learning to ask people to join you is an absolute prerequisite to effectively building a team and launching your church.

Understanding the *process* of launching a church is important, but it's even more important to understand the *people* side of a healthy launch. You must learn how to seek out the people God intends for you to work with if your first weekly service is to be successful.

Launch Team Versus Core Group

Launch Team: *A team of committed individuals who will assist you in preparing for and executing an effective launch. This is a team of people currently living in the area where your new church will meet—a team that you will build from scratch. The launch team is in existence only through the first weekly service.*

Your launch team has one singular purpose: to assist you in launching the church. When the launch service is over, the team dissipates. (Of course, hopefully the people won't go away, but their service in the church will shift to the weekly volunteers.) You may have heard the term "core group" applied to this initial team, but there is a big difference between a launch team and a core group. Many churches have sabotaged their launch by treating their launch team like a core group.

The basic idea behind a core group is to find 12 to 25 spiritually committed individuals in your area and convince them to help you start your church. This team then comes together in private or semiprivate meetings for three to six months to pray over and prepare for the new church. Undeniably, the team professes to be working together to start the church. However, core groups are built in such a way that their attention and intentions are often misguided.

Churches that only use the core-group process tend to start small and stay small. The reason has nothing to do with spiritual depth but rather with psychological laws: Individuals who meet together and work closely with each other for more than a couple of months will develop deep relationships and work to protect those relationships. In short, the group turns inward. This is not necessarily bad, unless you are trying to launch a church, which requires people to intentionally keep their focus on reaching out to others.

Launch Team		Core Group
A time-bound team		An open-ended team
Meets to plan the launch		Meets for spiritual growth
Involves anyone who is willing	VS.	Involves only the spiritually mature
Is engaged to accomplish a task		Is engaged to encourage and support
Focuses on those outside the church		Focuses on those in the group
Ends with an outward focus		Ends with an inward focus

In our experience with core groups, we have seen many solidify to the ultimate detriment of the church. We've heard comments from core-group members such as, "Pastor, why do we need to invite all these other people? We have such a great thing going. Why ruin it?" And, "Pastor, how are you going to meet my needs if so many others start coming?" Obviously, you don't want to develop a group that is going to be focused on their own growth rather than on sharing God's love with the community through your new church.

To ensure that your launch team does not start taking on the characteristics of a core group, you will have to fight the temptation to pastor the people on your team. That may seem counterintuitive to you, but you must understand that if you pastor the people on your launch team, you are making it less likely that you will ever pastor the people in your future church. Furthermore, never treat your launch team like a core group. It's not. While your team can pray together for the future church and even study the Bible or certain books on spiritual growth, the focus of the study and prayer should never be on the people in the group but on influencing those in the future church.

So, now that you know what a launch team is and is not, let's turn our attention to building it! Where do you find your team?

Building Your Launch Team

The first step in building your launch team is to identify who is already on it. If you are married, you and your spouse make two team members. If you have a worship leader, add him or her to your count. If your worship leader is married, add the spouse. That makes four. More than likely, this is your initial launch team. Ultimately, your team will grow, but it's important for you to truly comprehend that at this stage *you are the team*. Whether the team grows exponentially or stays relatively small, you are the base of the unit that will be working together to fulfill your God-given dream of starting an effective church.

Follow the Leader

If you are the lead or founding pastor, you need to step into the leadership position for your launch team. We have seen teams who started beautifully fail quickly because of the lack of a clear leader. Team leadership may be a new role for you, but it's one that you'll learn to embrace. By working on yourself and relying on God, you can develop the qualities essential to effective leadership (see appendix C for leadership resources).

Don't be fooled into thinking that being a solid leader undermines the spirit of teamwork. You can lead a team, hold people accountable and ensure that things get done in a way that fosters teamwork and gives glory to God. So get ready. It's time for you to step up. Everything that needs to be accomplished sits squarely on your shoulders. Don't shy away from leading. Even more important, don't surrender the vision of your church to others.

The single greatest tip that we can give you on how to effectively find and lead a team is to show people your heart before you ask for their hand. People want to know that you care, and they want to be part of something bigger than themselves. If you can articulate your vision in a way that excites people, they'll want to be on your team. If they respect the way that you relate to them and treat them, they will work hard for you. As Jesus taught, the greatest leader is the greatest servant. When you connect with people and seek to serve them through your position, you will be on the right track toward becoming an effective leader.

Begin with the End in Mind

As you think about building your launch team, ask yourself, *How many people do I need on this team by the time our church begins weekly services?* Working backward from your answer will help you determine how to build and structure your launch team. Let's take the following case study as an example.

FICTIONAL COMMUNITY CHURCH
A Team-Building Case Study for Lead Pastors

Jim is the lead pastor of Fictional Community Church (FCC), a new church that is four months from its September launch date. Right now, Jim's launch team is four people strong (Jim and his wife, his worship leader and his wife). Jim feels sure that he'll need to have 50 people on his team by September in order to launch as large as possible, which is, of course, his top priority. Since it's already May, he'd better get to work!

May:
Four months until launch / Two weeks
until first monthly service

Spring is in full swing, and Jim's first monthly service is just two weeks away. His four-person launch team has a clear leader (himself), and he's working toward a solid launch date of the second Sunday in September. Right now, though, Jim's pressure point is the first monthly service.

For this first monthly service, Jim and the other three members of his launch team will be taking care of everything: promoting the church, finding and securing a space, planning the service, purchasing equipment and printing programs. If Jim happens to meet someone along the way who wants to help his team prepare, all the better, but right now his initial team is taking the responsibility to see that things come together smoothly.

Jim knows that putting everything on the shoulders of this small launch team is a lot to ask, but the only other solution is to postpone starting the church. Since September is prime church-starting time, he knows he can't wait. Jim has partner churches in place, so he forges ahead and decides to hold at least four monthly services by September. (Jim also wants to get at least one monthly service in before school lets out, which is late May in the FCC community.)

For Jim, being totally responsible for the first monthly service has some great advantages. He is quickly becoming an expert on local businesses and is a familiar face around town. He is meeting printers, postal workers, marketing people and location coordinators. Not only that, but he's also learning firsthand exactly what it takes to make a service happen. So, when he has a larger launch team in place, he'll be able to train them from a position of experience.

May:
First monthly service and the week after

FCC's first monthly service is about to start. Jim and the other three team members are busy with final details—but not too busy to meet those who are arriving. People are actually coming in. Jim is ecstatic! The service begins with some worship songs. Jim remembers to ask people to fill out their communication cards (see chapter 8), and everything wraps up in about an hour. After the service, Jim and his team talk with attendees, scouting others who might be interested in being future launch-team members.

With the first service behind him, Jim thinks about all that he did wrong and all that he did right. To his surprise, 54 people had shown up. As usual, the count was a little off, so he calls it 51 in the report to his partner churches. Either way, it was more than the 50 he was praying for. Jim takes a little time to recover and celebrate what God has done—and then gets back to work.

The most important element of Jim's first service was not the offering, but the communication cards. So he and the launch team begin to go through the cards and handle follow-up. As Jim scans the communication cards and thinks about the people he met, he is on the lookout for possible launch team members. Specifically, here's what Jim is looking for:

- People who showed an above-average interest in FCC
- People who had warm smiles and pleasant personalities
- People who live in the community and represent his target demographic
- New Christians who have moved to the area
- People from his sponsoring churches who now live in the area
- College students
- People who may or may not have a relationship with God
- Disgruntled members from other local churches (*just kidding!*)

Seriously, Jim knows that he should avoid recruiting people from other churches at all costs. He is focused on starting a church for the *unchurched*. While people from other local churches may choose to attend, they are not prime candidates for his launch team. One member of his launch team was surprised that they were interested in bringing on people who may not yet be Christians. Jim explained that it's perfectly acceptable to have open-minded, personable nonbelievers on a launch team.

As Jim searches through the 30 or so cards that were turned in, he finds four that look like good prospects. Over the next three weeks, he'll follow up with these four people and invite them to help with the June service. If they all say yes, his launch team has doubled! If even two say yes, it has grown by 50 percent.

What will Jim ask these prospects to do?

- Come to next month's service early to help with set-up
- Serve in some capacity during the next month's service (help with refreshments, serve as greeters, assist in a technical area and so on)
- Volunteer other skills or connections that could help FCC have a healthy launch
- Give suggestions on improving their experience at FCC

Jim knows that God is putting people in his path who will be called to be on his launch team. He resists the fear that comes with asking because he understands that he is giving these individuals an opportunity to invest in the eternal work of God's kingdom through FCC.

June:
Three months until launch / One week until second monthly service

Two of the people that Jim followed up with said yes, and the team picked up another person when they e-mailed him after the last service. Thanks to the help of these three new team members, planning for the second service has become much easier than planning for the first. Now, Jim's seven-member launch team is about to meet at his house for some last minute preparation. Everyone is praying for 75 people to attend the June service. Jim can feel the excitement building!

June:
Second monthly service and the week after

Jim just wrapped up his second monthly service. As the crowd begins to thin out, the launch team is busy meeting everyone. There weren't 75 people there as Jim had hoped, but there was still a strong showing. Jim encourages the launch team to clean up the facility and reminds everyone of next Sunday night's debriefing. Out of the corner of his eye, Jim notices a couple from the service helping his wife with some cleanup. He makes a point to meet them and immediately senses that they could be future launch team members.

Cut to next Sunday night. Jim is sitting in his living room with the members of his emerging launch team—the seven from before and the wife from the couple that stayed late to help clean up (her husband is still at work and may show up a little later). Jim starts the meeting by asking the team four important questions:

1. What went right?
2. What went wrong?
3. What was missing?
4. What was confusing?

After asking all four questions, Jim sits back and lets his launch team answer (it's best if you ask all four questions at once and let people answer in any order). Once they've wrapped up their discussion, Jim assigns tasks for July's service preparation and closes the meeting with prayer. Jim then dismisses the four newer members of the launch team, while the other three initial members stay behind with him—there's still work to do.

Once again, Jim and the other three go through the communication cards and plan follow-up on possible launch team members. They come up with a list of 12, some who returned for the June service and some new people. Jim takes the majority of the names. Before saying goodnight, they make sure to celebrate the 66 people who attended this month's service.

July:
Two months until launch / One week until third monthly service

It's been a busy couple of weeks, but the results have been incredible. Jim has officially added 10 people to the launch team! There's so much growth that he had to move tonight's team meeting from his house to a nearby restaurant.

As Jim walks into the back dining room, he can hardly believe the sight—the room is filled with 15 people, and there are three more who couldn't make it. Once everyone has eaten, Jim walks them through the responsibilities for this coming Sunday. Again, the team is praying for 75 people to attend the service.

Throughout the rest of the week, Jim follows up with everyone to make sure responsibilities are being fulfilled and that everything is on track. A few of his team members drop the ball, so he has to work extra hard on Friday and Saturday to make sure that their tasks are finished. This is the life of a leader!

July:
Third monthly service and the week after

Having 18 people on his launch team has increased Jim's confidence—so much so that he announces a brief meeting following the service for anyone who might be interested in helping with the church's launch. He has set up a side room with some food, sign-up sheets and pens. After the service, Jim makes his way to the room and is floored by how full it is—and people are still coming in. He does his best to share about the upcoming launch, but frankly, he knows it's not his best presentation, as this is way more than expected! Again, the life of a leader . . .

Jim has decided to host a barbeque at his place in a couple of weeks, and he encourages everyone to sign up and attend. As the people leave, the existing launch team gives each person 10 "invite cards" that highlight the date of the next monthly service and feature a teaser for the teaching series that will begin on launch day. Several people hang around after the meeting to chat with Jim. One woman even jokes that the only reason she signed up for the barbeque is to see where the pastor lives (she may have been only half kidding). As the last person leaves and Jim collects the signup sheets, he hears a member of his launch team telling someone that she counted 83 people at the service.

The following week, Jim meets with the 18 members of his launch team to discuss July's service and prepare for the barbeque, August's monthly service and the quickly approaching launch.

Late July:
Barbeque at Jim's place

The grill is fired up and everyone seems to be having a good time. Jim and his wife have made a bet to see who can meet and remember the most people, so he's introducing himself left and right to the almost 30 people crammed into his backyard.

After the smoke clears from dinner, Jim calls everyone to attention. He takes this opportunity to share his calling (but not too much, he doesn't want to scare them) and cast some vision for FCC. Jim tells the crowd that he would like for each one of them to take part in August's service and to help with the launch. He identifies two or three possible roles that each person could take on and then asks them to indicate their interests on the information cards going around. They can sign up for a service team, or they can request more information on technical teams or the worship band.

When everyone leaves, Jim, his wife, the worship leader and his wife go through the cards. The worship leader takes the cards from the people who have expressed an interest in music or to be a part of the technical teams. Jim divides the rest of the cards evenly between himself and the other two. By the way, Jim's wife won that bet—by a landslide.

August:
Fourth monthly service and the week after

Jim stares in awe at the FCC worship band. Okay, it's not a full band yet, but it's much bigger than it was last month. And there are a lot of people serving that he doesn't even know! (Along with winning the bet, it looks as if Jim's wife got most of the people she met to agree to serve.) This service is definitely shaping up to be the best one yet.

During the service, Jim challenges everyone to invite 10 of their friends to come with them to the next month's launch.

He's doing the math in his head: If there are 100 people at this service (which is what it looks like), it could mean a potential 1,000 people at the launch! Jim feels his heart start to race, and he quickly moves to the next announcement—inviting everyone to a picnic in the park on the Saturday eight days before the launch.

After the service, Jim interrupts the teardown to congratulate everyone who served. He challenges them once again to invite their friends to the launch on Sunday. He also remembers to invite them to next week's launch team meeting, the next-to-last meeting of its kind!

August's postservice launch team meeting puts 40 people back in Jim's backyard. He leads them through final details on the picnic comeback event and goes through each of the launch-Sunday details. As the meeting is wrapping up, one of the men Jim has seen quite a bit of (but who has never spoken up before) reminds everyone how important their involvement is. He uses the words "making history" when talking about the start of FCC. Those words stay with Jim.

After the meeting, Jim and a half-dozen team members go through the 82 cards from the August service (which had a total of 121 people in attendance) and select a few people who could be potential future launch team members. If the 40 who attended tonight are any indication, Jim should hit his goal of 50 members by launch Sunday.

September:
Picnic in the park / Eight days until launch

The storm clouds are gathering just before the picnic start time, but Jim and his team are still giving it 100 percent and praying for a strong turnout. Despite the light drizzle, people start showing up. Ultimately, the heavy rain holds off, and it turns out to be a good afternoon—even if not quite what Jim had hoped for. Yet Jim knows that even when things don't go perfectly, God is still at work. He moves past his slight disappointment over the picnic and jumps into getting ready for the launch. Seven days and counting!

September:
One day until launch

At the last minute, Jim finds out that he will be able to get into his worship space on the Saturday before the launch. He quickly calls everyone on his now 50-plus launch team and changes the Saturday meeting location from his house to the "church." About 41 people show up (okay, it's 41 exactly). After the poor showing at last week's picnic, Jim is becoming obsessed about counting—maybe too obsessed. He talks through the next day's service and nervously reminds everyone of the goal he shared a month ago of having 250 people in attendance on launch day. After a powerful time of prayer, several team members remain to do whatever advance set-up they can.

September:
Launch Sunday!

FCC's launch day is here. This is where this case study ends. In real life, we have seen the above scenario play out with an initial attendance of anywhere from 100 to 300 people. In fact, some of the largest launches in the history of American church planting are now happening. If you follow the proper launch process, your church can end up being a successful case study of its own!

Three Top Launch-Team Temptations

As you work the launch process, you will face three major temptations. Each temptation is specifically designed to keep you from launching at maximum capacity. Make sure you understand the reality of these temptations so that you will be able to stand against them when they come.

Temptation #1: Change the Launch Schedule

As we mentioned in chapter 6, you may be tempted to change the launch schedule when things do not go as planned. When your launch process is delivering better than expected results, you may be tempted to move the launch to an earlier date. Likewise, if your process is not bringing the results you had hoped for, you may be tempted to adjust the schedule and push your launch later.

Don't give in to this all-too-common temptation. If you heard from God in selecting your date, stay the course. There will always be a reason to change your schedule, but no reason is good enough. Don't forget, God is omniscient. He knew every circumstance you would face along the way when He led you to your original launch date. Don't short-circuit His best.

Temptation #2: Give Your Launch Team Too Much Control

If you work the launch team process properly, you will likely attract some heavy hitters. Christians or not, these successful people may be experts in their field—perhaps financial experts who want to jump in and fund your church, marketing experts who want to take over that area to relieve some of your stress, or even strategy experts who think they can give you a better development plan.

Having experts on your team can't hurt . . . unless you give them too much control. Many a church planter thinks he can hand over an area and manage it closely, only to find out down the line that giving over the power was a big mistake. You can never give up the vision God has given you to others, even if they are experts in their field. Yes, your experts may know a lot about their particular field, but you are the expert on your church and the vision that God has given to you. Listen to their advice and heed their insights, but don't give them control over what God has appointed you to lead.

Temptation #3: Merge with Another Church

This temptation may confront you in a couple of different ways. Perhaps a struggling church will hear about your new church and approach you with a brilliant plan for why merging would be beneficial to you both. We have one word of advice for you: *Run!* Or perhaps another church will offer you the use of their building. No matter how good the proposition looks on paper, don't do it. God has something better in store just for you and your church.

Both expressions of Temptation #3 have long strings attached. We have seen more church plants ruined prelaunch by this temptation than by the other two combined. If you find yourself facing this temptation in either form, ask, "If I had an additional $100,000, $500,000 or $1 million, would I even consider the possibility?" The answer is always no. That's exactly what you should say to this temptation.

Launching for Legacy

We've said it before: A healthy launch is the single greatest indicator of future church health. The last two chapters have given you a proven process for launching healthy and launching large. Here are a few final guidelines for ensuring a healthy launch:

- Don't do a membership class until after your launch.

- Do everything possible to keep your launch team outwardly focused. If you think you are doing enough, you're not.

- The launch team is not a democracy. Don't vote. You are the leader. Lead.

- Remember that your launch team is a time-limited, purpose-driven team. It ends with the debriefing session following your launch. At that meeting, release the launch team members to join a ministry team of their choice.

- The launch team will force you to learn how to manage teams. Keep those lessons with you. Everything about church involves managing teams of people.

- Preparing a launch team to maximize your first service is first and foremost a spiritual enterprise. Pray and fast—a lot.

Here is a truth that you as a church planter need to accept now to save yourself a lot of hurt and disappointment in the future: Your launch team will not stay with you over the long haul. Many church planters make the mistake of thinking that the people from their launch team (whom they have grown to love) will be the same people who will grow the church with them in the long term. That is seldom, if ever, the case.

At The Journey, we had a launch team of over 30 people. The team was phenomenal, and we were close to every member. However, just three years later, not a single person from that launch team was still at The Journey! Some of the people on our launch team were members of other churches who were simply helping us get started. Some became disillusioned with the church as we began to grow larger and reach new people. Most of our original team simply moved out of the city in the years following our launch.

While it's sad to see people go, it's part of God's process in growing your church. So, expect it, be prepared for it, and be thankful that you have the opportunity to serve with so many different people at different points along the journey.

Setting the Solid Foundation

Have you ever watched a contractor pour the concrete that is to become the foundation of a house? Before they pour, they prepare the ground, define the boundaries of the slab area and position themselves to supervise the flow. Then, when the concrete trucks start pouring, the workers don't let the concrete pile up. They are constantly spreading it out and adding water to keep it from setting too early, because once that concrete hardens, it's virtually impossible to expand the foundation.

The launch process for your church is similar. Your launch date and monthly service schedule define the boundaries. Your launch team is the poured concrete that will form the actual foundation. You water and spread the foundation by keeping the launch team outwardly focused as you all work toward the launch. Your most important job is to make sure that the mix does not set until that foundation is large enough to build your church on. A strong launch team that builds to a successful launch is the foundation for effectively starting a church.

It is like a person who builds a house on a strong foundation laid upon the underlying rock. When the floodwaters rise and break against the house, it stands firm because it is well built.

LUKE 6:48

Implementation

Wow, you are actually still reading this book, and we are pretty close to the end. And to think, our publisher said no one would read this far! Anyway, the best is yet to come.

In the next few chapters, we are going to look at what you should do after your launch so that your church can just keep on doing what you were called to do in the first place: reach people, disciple people and move them toward maturity. In the final chapter, we will discuss having an unshakable conviction about your church's growth so that you can remove the barriers that the enemy might put in your way.

So grab another grande soy nonfat splenda-sweetened double latte and jump in.

Top 10 Most Unexpected Reactions from Those Who Have Read This Far

1. "I feel that I'm a little bit dumber for having read this book."
   —Pastor Joe, Naperville, IL

2. "Better than *The Purpose Driven Life*! Nelson was not nearly this smart when he served as a pastor on my staff."
   —Pastor Rick Warren, Lake Forest, CA

3. "If you only read one book this year, read something by Erwin McManus. If you need something to balance your coffee table, get this book." —Pastor Ted, Cleveland, OH

4. "Just like Andy Stanley without the intelligent ideas or clear presentation." —Pastor John, Alpharetta, GA

5. "This is a great guide to planting tomatoes or squash. Planting churches? Heck no, not this book!" —Pastor Luis, Homestead, FL

6. "My good friends Milton and Derrick have written a great book. I know these guys, and you should buy this book."
   —Pastor Dan, Wichita, KS

7. "This book will help you grow a great church like Willow Creek or Saddleback. Only with less people and far less impact."
   —Pastor Jake, Schaumburg, IL

8. "We have prayed for years for God to plant a great church in New York City. I'm still praying."
   —Rev. Richards, Denominational Mission Board, Henderson, TN

9. "When I heard that Nelson and Kerrick were going to start a church, I said, 'Get out of town!' I meant it then and I mean it now." —Pastor Titus, New York, NY

10. "You know how Ed Young, Jr., is entertaining, exciting and cutting edge? Yeah, these guys are nothing like that."
    —Pastor Raul, Seattle, WA

11. "I read it once. I read it twice. I read it a third time. I still have no idea what they're talking about."
    —Pastor Mitch, Oklahoma City, OK

Reaching People

Passion. What does that word make you think of? Christ's suffering and ministry before the crucifixion? Or maybe a powerful emotion, like love, joy or excitement? Isn't it interesting that both of these are legitimate definitions for the word?

Scholars have argued that the sufferings of Jesus are called the Passion because of His powerful, emotional commitment to the cup that had been set before Him. Seeing this common word through the lens of Christ's final hours brings an entirely new hue to its definition for believers, especially for church planters. Just as Jesus was emotionally and powerfully committed to fulfilling His Passion, you are called to reflect the same passion in starting your church from scratch. And what is the driving force of your passion as you set out on this journey? The all-consuming desire to reach people with God's truth.

> [Jesus] said to his disciples, "The harvest is so great, but the workers are so few. So pray to the Lord who is in charge of the harvest; ask him to send out more workers for his fields" (Matt. 9:37-38).

Everything we have discussed so far is designed to help you be an effective worker in His fields and to help you reach as many people as possible through your new church. Your calling, your strategy, your fundraising and your launching process are all designed to help you bring in the harvest of new believers. If you are not passionate about bringing new people into God's kingdom, you may need to reevaluate your decision to be a church planter. The Passion—His and ours for His—is what drives the church planter who has been truly called by the Lord.

Passion and Enthusiasm

Passion for reaching people breeds a God-filled enthusiasm, and enthusiasm is an essential ingredient in reaching new people. When you have an attitude of enthusiasm, those around you become enthusiastic. They respond to your energy and are eager to hear what you have to say. Dr. David Schwartz has studied the effects of enthusiasm in various arenas. He notes:

> A man who lacks enthusiasm never develops it in another. But a person who is enthusiastic soon has enthusiastic followers . . . The enthusiastic teacher need never worry about disinterested students. The activated minister need never be distressed by a sleepy congregation . . . To activate others, to get them to be enthusiastic, you must first be enthusiastic yourself.[1]

With the proper passion for reaching people, how could we, as church planters, not be enthusiastic? It's up to us to keep the level of passion high and the enthusiasm turned toward those outside the doors of our new church.

When we started The Journey, we were consumed with issues of evangelism. To this day, we spend a lot of our time exploring the subject. Our call is and has always been to reach new people. Period. In those early days, quite frankly, we didn't have a clue what might work. We were running on faith, passion and enthusiasm. While we are still students of evangelism, we have learned some things along the way that can help focus outreach enthusiasm into effective evangelism.

Finding Focus

If we asked you, "Who are you trying to reach?" you would most likely respond, "Well, everyone, of course!" While it's true that you want to share the gospel with as many people as possible, you will need to develop a clear picture of the specific demographic your new church is targeting in order to effectively reach the greatest number of people. Diffused light has little impact, but focused light has the ability to cut through steel. Take time to *focus* so that you are able to reach the specific people God has called you to. Make sure that your focus population is:

- *Findable*: They shouldn't be hard to pinpoint but evident from demographic research.

- *Outward-Oriented*: They should not be the result of an inward, or comfort, mentality.

- *Community-Based*: They should be a significant part of your local community.

- *Unreached*: They should be an as-yet-unreached segment of that community.

- *Specific*: You should be able to specifically define your focus demographic to anyone.

To zero in on this *focus* population, you will need to ask yourself the following three questions.

1. Who Are the Key Population Groups Living in My Area?

Do some demographic research. Don't just go with what you see. What are the dominant age groups in your area? Are there more singles or more families with kids? If you have lived in your area for a while, you will be at a disadvantage when it comes to answering these questions. It has been proven that once you live in an area for an extended period of time, you don't really see the area as it is. Instead, you only see your small corner and project that personal reality on the whole area.

When we first moved to Manhattan, we thought it would be good to do some research by questioning several long-time residents on basic demographic information. We asked them questions such as, "Who lives in this neighborhood?" and "What types of people have been here the longest?" In response, they told us which particular age groups were moving in or out of the city and which ethnic groups were on the rise or decline. They also gave some other information on basic trends they had observed.

In almost every instance, the information they gave us was wrong! The actual demographic studies showed something completely different from what they had told us. We learned the hard way that the perceptions of residents aren't the best indicator of what is happening in a particular area. So get the facts.

2. What Population Group Is Not Being Reached Effectively? This question is critical. Once you have an understanding of the dominant people groups in your area, try to find out what populations are not being embraced by other churches. This can be tricky. You've probably heard it said, as we have, that no county in America is truly churched. So, you could argue that everyone in your area is unreached—and, most likely, you'd be correct.

Yet there are definitely groups that are more unreached than others. Perhaps a housing boom has recently attracted young couples. Maybe a certain ethnic population has just moved in. While people in every demographic ultimately need to be churched, you will be more effective if you can incorporate your new church plant with a population trend that is on the rise and represent people that are not otherwise being reached.

One of the big demographic trends in Manhattan from 1990 to 2000, the decade just prior to our starting The Journey, was the gentrification of large portions of the city. Some have argued that gentrification (the process of upper-class professional development in a formerly urban area) is bad, while many others have argued the opposite. Good or bad, this gentrification was bringing a huge influx of young professionals into Manhattan. As we observed the trend, we realized that very few churches in Manhattan were focused on reaching this new demographic. Most had entrenched programs that had been created for an outdated demographic and showed no desire to revamp. Not only did this reality affirm our call to the city, it also brought focus to our evangelism efforts.

3. What Population Group Do I Best Relate To?

Of the various demographics in your area, to what population do you best relate? Careful here. We are not asking what population you want to reach or to what population do you feel a special connection. Rather, we are asking to what population you best *relate*. There can be a difference. You will best relate to people like you or to people who are similar but slightly younger than you are. You may have a heart for a different population group, but that doesn't mean you are called or equipped to reach them. Answer this question with the honesty and integrity it requires.

The Sweet Spot

The point at which these three questions intersect is your sweet spot. After examining each of the three questions for The Journey, we came to realize that our focus would be the young professionals moving to Manhattan in droves. The demographic was evident and a fast-growing part of our community; further, they were unreached, and we could relate to them.

By defining our focus, we discovered a group of people that we could effectively and enthusiastically reach. Of course, young professionals were not the only group of people that could have demanded our attention. There are certainly large numbers of other unreached people in New York City. However, at the intersection of the answers to these three questions, our focus was clear.

What happens when the sweet spot comes as a genuine surprise? Some of the hardest conversations we've had with potential church planters have been when the planter clearly didn't match the people he wanted to reach. Yet when the three questions above are not answered honestly, the result can be disappointing—even disastrous.

At one conference, I (Nelson) met a very committed man who was near the end of his ministry. He passionately shared with me how his heart was breaking for an emerging generation in a remote area of the city where he lived. Since no one else was stepping up, he was thinking of starting a church there. However, when I asked him the three questions above, he began to realize that although he had a big heart for this emerging population, he just couldn't relate to them. He decided not to move ahead as a lead planter and to pray for God to send someone that he could come alongside of and assist.

Very few ministers have a gifting for cross-cultural ministry. If you don't relate to the population you feel called to reach, pray for God to be especially clear that He's calling you to this people. Or pray for God to send a person who does relate, and then support him or her with all you've got.

Timing Is Everything

Now that you know your focus demographic, what's the best time to reach them? Your burning enthusiasm for evangelism may lead you to believe that anytime is a good time to reach people. But, in truth, people are most open to the gospel during three specific periods of life: (1) *trouble*, (2) *tension* and (3) *transition*.

Think through what these periods will look like in your demographic. What troubles might your focus group be experiencing? What kinds of tension are common to those you are trying to reach? When do they undergo transition, and what kind? By way of example, here's how we examined our focus population in light of these periods:

Troubles Faced by Young Professionals in Manhattan:
- Loss of job
- Sickness
- Debt
- Guilt
- Relationship trouble

Tensions Faced by Young Professionals in Manhattan:
- Finding a job
- Meeting the demands of their job
- Work/life balance issues
- Paying the bills
- Loneliness/lack of true friendships
- Distance from family

Transitions Faced by Young Professionals in Manhattan:
- Moving from small town to big city
- Transitioning from being a student to having a career
- Moving from depending on Mom and Dad to being independent
- Living alone to living with a roommate
- Moving from college to the city

- Being single to being married
- Being married to being single

We could go further and customize these lists for the different segments of our young professional population. The troubles, tensions and transitions would be different for married people than they would be for singles and different for corporate professionals than for professional artists. You get the picture. When you shape your evangelism efforts around life circumstances that cause reciprocity, you'll be all the more effective in opening your focus group to your message.

Bring It into Focus

By applying the realities of your focus population to some of the concepts we've discussed (such as your marketing, your monthly services and your comeback events), you are setting your church up to have incredible influence.

Marketing

If your focus group is a young, hip crowd, your marketing should be young and hip. If you are in a retirement community in Florida, your marketing pieces should have larger print. Subtle changes based on your target can be of the utmost importance. And remember, marketing is more than just printed materials. It includes your website and anything else that is visible to the public.

When I first designed The Journey's website, I was living in Southern California. Without sensing the danger ahead,

I asked a designer from California to help me with the initial site. Now, I knew a lot about New York, but I neglected some important principles about addressing our focus population. For example, I knew that young professionals in Manhattan generally wore dark colors and that most of the websites aimed at this demographic used dark colors as well.

However, forgetting everything I knew about matching my target group, I worked with this Californian designer to build a bright, beautiful website full of sunny colors. Wrong! The website was perfect for Californians but was a big mismatch for the Manhattan crowd. (If you want to have some fun, use "the way back machine" www.archive.org to see the various evolutions of www.nyjourney.com.) Although our website can always use improvement, it now matches our focus population much more accurately.

Your Monthly Services

As mentioned earlier, your monthly services should speak to your focus group. This includes the type of music you use and the message content you choose. Music styles within the church have been a huge source of controversy in recent years. Our belief is that your music should speak to the primary group you are trying to reach.

That being said, I have a confession to make. I like country music, but country music isn't cool—at least not in New York City. The vast majority of people in my focus population would rather listen to nails on a chalkboard than have to sit through a country song. So, we've never done a "countryesque" worship song at The Journey, and we probably never will. It simply wouldn't catalyze worship for our focus demographic. It's not about my personal musical preferences; it's about the people we are trying to reach.

In the same way, you should preach on topics related to your focus population. If you are hoping to reach young families, kicking off a parenting series on launch Sunday would be a great idea. We've discovered that a relationship series geared toward your demographic is probably the best way to launch a new church. Remember, you will want to do a loosely connected message series during your monthly services and then kick off a big attraction series at your launch. Both message series should be attractive and relevant to your focus population.

Comeback Events

Being sensitive to your focus population will also help you in planning the comeback events you hold between your monthly services. These events should be activities that are familiar to and fun for your focus population. If people in your area aren't used to backyard barbeques, maybe your people are naturally more open to a formal dinner at someone's home or a well-known restaurant.

For added impact, consider piggybacking your comeback events with other events your focus population is already planning to attend. As we mentioned, early on we planned some comeback events around the opening of certain movies. New Yorkers see films. Since they were going to go to the movies anyway, why not plan to go together and do dinner afterward?

Build It and They Will Come . . . Right?

What if you plan an event or an actual service and the people don't show up? You won't be alone. It has happened to the best of us and will probably, at some point, happen to you. Don't get too discouraged. No one ever said reaching people would be easy.

You've probably heard the saying, "Experience is the best teacher." Well, that's only half true. *Evaluated* experience is the best teacher. So if you find yourself in this situation, use it as a time of evaluation. Ask yourself, *What went right? What went wrong? What was missing? What was confusing?* Pray and ask God to teach you through the experience. Reevaluate everything and put together another plan. Most important, try again. If God has called you to this endeavor, you'll never be down for the count.

Our first monthly service wasn't exactly a huge success. While the room felt fairly full—we had mission teams from other churches in attendance—we only attracted 13 true prospects from Manhattan. In a sense, we were encouraged. At least someone had shown up! On the other hand, we realized that it was only 13 people. As we evaluated, prayed, evaluated some more and prayed some more, God turned our discouragement into gratefulness. We saw that we needed to focus on and be grateful for the people that God had sent us instead of wasting energy worrying about those elusive people who weren't there. An agonizing lesson indeed, but one we've never forgotten.

How about this one: What if the people you want to reach don't show up, but another group does? We have seen church planters put a lot of effort into attracting a certain demographic only to look up and realize that a totally different type of crowd is attending. For example, perhaps you were trying to reach career-minded singles, but instead you attracted a much larger proportion of young married couples. This may not be a problem. Instead, it may be a godly correction of your strategy. (You did leave room for God to show up in your strategy, didn't you?)

Here's where our thinking differs slightly from the traditional view of targeting: If you target a certain focus population but end up reaching a different population, simply adjust to this new population. Make your target the people you are reaching. After all, as long as you are attracting the unchurched, does an age difference or demographic difference really matter that much? Our guess is that God is guiding you into the right "sweet spot."

On the other hand, if you want to reach the unchurched but only the churched are showing up, you may actually have a problem. Reevaluate your communications to see if you are using too much insider language. You might want to read *The Purpose Driven Church* by Rick Warren, especially the sections on "Reaching Your Community" and "Attracting a Crowd," and examine whether you've violated some of the principles he details in addressing the topic of how to reach the unchurched.

Five Ideas for Reaching People

Now that you know who your focus population is and how to best effectively reach out to them, let's recap some of the tips for getting them to your monthly services and your launch.

1. Direct Marketing

As we mentioned previously, direct mail is one of the most cost-effective ways to get word out about your church. People are being more creative with direct mail than ever before. From using oversized mailers to delivering the mailers via nontraditional routes (such as inside newspapers or through door hangers), there's still a lot to be explored in this area.

2. Mission Teams

While it's true that mission teams require a lot of energy and preplanning, we have always found the results to be well worth the effort. Mission teams from your sponsor churches can help you with comeback events, serve at your monthly services and prayer-walk your community. More important, these teams can perform servant evangelism outreach.

3. Servant Evangelism

Servant evangelism is a great way to serve your community and introduce people to your new church by showing God's love in a practical way. We highly recommend that every church planter read Steve Sjogren's writings on servant evangelism. Start with his book *Conspiracy of Kindness*, and then pick up one of his newer books—such as his church-planting book *Community of Kindness*.

On a hot day in the park, what do sweaty joggers and rollerbladers need? Bottled water, of course! One of our favorite servant evangelism projects at The Journey is to hand out bottles of water along with information about our church. We load up each of our volunteers with a case of water from a local wholesale club and a stack of postcards about The Journey, and then strategically position them around the park.

In servant evangelism, the first goal is to serve people. We give them something practical that they can immediately appreciate.

Obviously, we want them to read the accompanying postcard, but our goal is to serve first and invite second. We have repeated this scenario hundreds of times, and each time it produces fruit, bringing about 30 percent of The Journey's first-time guests. (Visit www.churchfromscratch.com to see our top 10 favorite servant evangelism projects and find out more on how we have applied Steve Sjogren's approach. You can also visit Steve's website at www.servantevangelism.com.)

4. Events

Over the years, The Journey has had a love/hate relationship with events, both single and multi-sponsor. We have done events that were hugely successful and attracted tons of people, and we have also poured buckets of energy into events that totally fizzled. After the latter type, we always find ourselves asking if we should continue to do events. Our conclusion? Most definitely. Events have always allowed us to personally introduce our church to large numbers of people. They will do the same for you.

5. People Inviting People

While direct mail, mission teams, servant evangelism and events are all wildly useful, don't ever focus on these to the exclusion of simple friend-to-friend evangelism. Although personal invitation won't bring in the crowds, it is truly one of the most effective modes of outreach. The key is for you to provide relevant, simple, nonthreatening ways for your launch team and those already attending your church to invite their friends.

Some of the best ideas we've come across include:

- Handing 100 door hangers to everyone on your launch team for them to distribute in their neighborhoods before the next monthly service
- Giving everyone 10 invite postcards to hand out for your next monthly service or comeback event
- Challenging people at the prelaunch services to list the names of 10 to 15 friends on a sheet of paper who they will invite to the launch
- Training your launch team to pray for and invite their friends to church
- Leading the way personally by inviting your friends to church

From the outset of your new church, create a culture of outward focus and person-to-person evangelism. By doing so, you'll establish a foundation on which you can build a strong community.

Reaching People for the Kingdom

You are starting a church because there are people who need to be reached. Any other reason is sub par. You have been given an incredible opportunity and responsibility to bring people into the knowledge of Jesus Christ. Hold Jesus' words from the Parable of the Faithful Servant as inspiration:

> The master was full of praise. "Well done, my good and faithful servant. You have been faithful in handling this small amount, so now I will give you many more responsibilities. Let's celebrate together!" (Matt. 25:21).

As you start reaching people—whether one, ten, hundreds or thousands—if you are faithful, God will send you more. If you are passionate and diligent about reaching the unreached, there will come a time when the number of people who attend your launch service will be the average number of first-time guests at your church on any given Sunday. God wants His kingdom to overflow, and He's called you to be part of making that happen. Reach out passionately everywhere you can and watch as He blesses you with more outreach opportunities than you could have ever imagined!

> As your name deserves, O God, you will be praised
> to the ends of the earth.
>
> PSALM 48:10

Note

1. David Schwartz, *The Magic of Thinking Big* (New York: Fireside Publishing, 1987), n.p.

Building Systems

When the person in line next to you has a hacking cough, aren't you thankful that your digestive system works? Wait, no, that's your immune system, right? The digestive system couldn't serve the same purpose as the immune system any more than the endocrine system could fill our lungs with air. The same is true for any of the systems in our body—if one fails, we'll find ourselves in a predicament. But when each does its job, we are healthy. Each system has an essential task to complete, in a specified manner, so that the rest of the body can continue to function properly.

Just as our bodies are made up of interdependent systems, so is the church. The systems you put in place from the beginning are the essential processes that will help it remain healthy and give it the ability to develop. The healthier the systems are, the healthier the church will be, and the larger it will be able to grow.

> For as we have many members in one body, but all the members do not have the same function, so we, being many, are one body in Christ, and individually members of one another (Rom. 12:4-5, *NKJV*).

So, what exactly is a "church system"? How does it function? A church system is simply a strategic process that **S**aves **Y**ou **S**tress, **T**ime, **E**nergy and **M**oney. Just as the skeletal system provides a framework for our bodies, initial church systems provide structure for a new church. When it comes to establishing healthy systems, you have an advantage in launching from scratch—you get to build the systems without being tied to any traditional ways of doing things. But with this opportunity comes great responsibility. You must be careful about what systems you establish and how and when you establish them, as they will become a part of the foundation of your new church.

Baby Steps

When you came screaming into this world, you were only ready to deal with essential systems—namely, those critical to your body's development. If your parents had tried to introduce you to the educational system when you were six months old, you wouldn't have been able to process it. You still needed to develop the basics before moving on to more advanced systems for your continued growth. In the same way, when building systems for your new church, don't try to establish everything in the beginning. You can't do it all at once. Just as you had to put your muscular system to the test on all fours before you could walk and then run, your church needs to gain and exercise strength before moving too far. In reality, there are only a handful of systems that you need to implement during the first year of a new church's existence.

Build your initial systems properly and you will have a healthy base that will enable you to do many great things in the years to come. Try to do it all at once and you'll stretch yourself too thin, ending up with an anemic church. If you compare the systems in your church to the ministries of your church, you will see a similarity. Do a few ministries well in the beginning and you will be able to add many more ministries down the road.

We've always been dreamers. When we started The Journey, we had big dreams for countless ministry opportunities. One of those dreams was to have a strong community ministry that would feed the homeless, serve at-risk kids and provide housing for the poor. But during our first year, we did very little with community ministry other than an occasional message about meeting the needs of our city or a single event in which we served alongside a local community ministry program. Why? We understood that during the first couple of years we needed to focus on building the Sunday service and the other basic systems of the church. We had to learn the alphabet before we could move to diagramming sentences. We waited a year and a half before we launched our community ministry, and even then, it still took another year for that ministry system to become sustainable.

But it was more than worth it! Now we have people feeding the hungry, clothing the poor and providing for basic needs of our city every week. We learned this truth in action: Focus on the basics in the first year and you can do even more in the second.

First-Year Systems

There are eight systems that you should focus on during the first year of your new church:

1. The Sunday service
2. Evangelism and Assimilation 101
3. The church's website
4. Baptism
5. Recordkeeping and databases
6. Basic accounting
7. Corporate/legal structure
8. Leadership development

Everything else can wait 8 to 18 months, depending on how things develop. Yes, *everything* else. Start with the basics.

The Sunday Service

We don't need to tell you how important the Sunday service is. It is the front door of your church. In small ways, you'll begin developing your Sunday service system early on through your monthly services. Then, once you launch your church, the Sunday service system should become a primary focus. Moving from monthly to weekly services can be a rude awakening. You plan your first weekly service for months, and then as soon as it's over, there's another one in six days! Be prepared for the change of pace so that you aren't caught off guard.

Without an effective Sunday service system in place, it's all too easy to get caught up in the Sunday rat race and become so focused on preparing for each week's service that you don't have energy left for anything else. Despite all of your focused time and attention, if this occurs, the quality of the service will eventually begin to decline. While it's natural to pour yourself into each Sunday service for the first two or three months, this type of pressure will quickly become a major energy and ministry drain. An effective Sunday service system should **S**ave **Y**ou **S**tress, **T**ime, **E**nergy and **M**oney.

So how do you develop an effective Sunday system? Here are some basics:

- If you are in rented facilities, develop a solid load-in and load-out process. Continually ask yourself, *How can we do this better and in less time?*

- Make a list of everything you are doing for Sunday, evaluate it, and then ask, "What's on this list that we could mobilize volunteers to accomplish?" Model each task well yourself and then quickly give it away.

- Hire a $50-a-week staff person to assist with some of the most energy-draining or time-consuming Sunday preparations.

- Condense the worship order preparation time for each upcoming Sunday. For the worship leader, this means selecting the songs earlier in the week. For the teaching pastor, this means having an outline or clear direction about a message earlier in the week. When we first started, our initial goal was to have the worship order by Friday at noon. But little by little during the first year, we shortened this deadline to Thursday and then to Wednesday.

- Plan your preaching calendar in advance. If you know where you are going with next week's or next month's teaching, you'll be able to plan much more effectively (see www.churchfromscratch.com for a free resource to help with this).

Take these basic guidelines, sit down with your worship leader and key volunteers, and start brainstorming ways to improve every aspect of your Sunday preparation. Sunday is the most important day in the life of your church, and it deserves a system that will maximize its impact. By creating an effective Sunday service system, you will be able to raise the quality of the weekly service while shortening the amount of time it takes to achieve such quality. And that is a recipe for unlimited ministry expansion.

Evangelism and Assimilation 101

As you begin to build a quality Sunday service system, you will start attracting the unreached to your church. Remember Jesus' words in Matthew 25:21: "You have been faithful in handling this small amount, so now I will give you many more responsibilities." A basic evangelism and assimilation system is the process that allows you to be faithful with the small amount so that God can bless you with more.

To start developing the evangelism side of this two-pronged system, you'll need to ask yourself the following questions:

- How does someone explore or express a decision to follow Christ at our church? Does he or she check a box on the communication card? Does he or she talk with someone after the service? How can we make the process as clear as possible?

- What do we say, share or give to a person who is making a first-time decision to follow Christ? Do we need to have New Christian Packets at the Sunday service? Are we going to mail the new believer something? How can we help this person clarify his or her decision?

- How can we help the new Christian get plugged into our church? How do we help him or her meet people, start serving and start growing?

These questions just scratch the surface of your evangelism outreach, but they'll be helpful as you start building a system to care for the new believers that God will send your way. Perhaps the most important part of this system is for you and your staff to pray for these new Christians and to take personal responsibility for their growth.

Evangelism and assimilation go hand in hand. In fact, many times, assimilation precedes evangelism because unreached people will often attend for quite a while before making a decision to follow Christ. In thinking through your basic assimilation process, ask yourself:

- How do we know who is a first-time guest each Sunday? How do we collect his or her contact information?

- Are we making our service easy for a first timer to attend? Does that person know where to enter, check in his or her kids, find the restroom, and so on?

- How are we following up on first-time guests? (See appendix C for information on the Assimilation Seminar.)

Henry Ford said, "Before everything else, getting ready is the secret of success." Preparation paves the way back to your doorstep for your first-time guests. But if you aren't ready to serve them properly the first time they show up, you may never see them again. Be prepared. Establish a system to help you invest in those whom God sends your way.

The Church's Website

We live in a web-oriented society. Without the Internet, most of us don't know how to find directions or look up a phone number. We've all become quickly dependent. As a result, many church planters are tempted to go overboard with their website during the first year and waste huge amounts of time and money. This is not a smart system. When it comes to your website, less is more during the prelaunch stage through the end of year one. An award-winning website with all the bells and whistles will add very little to your church's growth (numerically or spiritually) during the first year.

What's important is minimal content framed by a quality look that will be inviting to your focus population. Include only the following:

- Where your church meets
- What time you meet
- Directions to the church's location
- What to expect at the service

· A little bit about you and any staff
· A short history of the church

Anything beyond that is not needed, even if you are starting a church in Silicon Valley. In particular, here are a few things that you should not include on your website:

· Too many pictures of the lead pastor
· Too many pictures of the lead pastor's spouse
· Music of any kind
· "Under construction" signs—just leave the area out
· Anything that takes a long time to load on a slower connection
· Insider language that only seminary grads understand
· Your personal blog
· Anything poorly written or of poor quality
· Outdated content
· Links to your favorite websites

We are amazed at the number of church websites we visit that contain high-powered graphics, intricate coding and in-depth Bible teaching tools yet fail to mention their service times and location. The most visited pages of a church planter's website are those that provide information about the service and information about the pastor. Stick with the basics, and keep whatever content you do post updated.

Simple, informative and easy are the keys to this system. People want to be able to jump on and find the information they need without a hassle. Don't let simplicity suffer for the sake of your technological vision.

Baptism

Baptism can be one of the most exciting celebrations in a new church because you actually get to see tangible results of all of your prayer and efforts. In the first four years of The Journey, around 300 people took the step to be baptized. On several occasions, we have seen close to 50 people baptized on a single day. While those days are incredibly thrilling, perhaps the most unforgettable baptism at The Journey was the very first one that we held.

In August 2002, 20 Journey folks trekked out to a Long Island beach for the church's first baptism. One person was being baptized, but you better believe that we celebrated that one life change with all the excitement it deserved! I (Kerrick) will never forget lifting this young man (who subsequently gave his life to serving with a Christian mission agency) out of the frigid coastal water and hearing the cheers of celebration and encouragement from the members of our young church. Here was a tangible sign that God was at work! Even today, we still look back on that Long Island baptism as one of the most important days in the history of The Journey.

As you begin to think about the system of baptism, we would like to extend a challenge to you: Take a stand against boring baptism services! Baptisms are celebrations of life change and need to be maximized as such. The first baptism in a church can be a great way to build momentum and celebrate what God has done so far.

There's no hard and fast rule on when to do your first baptism, but we suggest that you wait at least until you've started regular weekly services—not during monthly services or on launch Sunday. Some churches are able to do their first baptism three or four months into weekly services; others have to wait longer. For now, put a couple of possible dates on your calendar and see what God does. You will know when the time is right. In the meantime, ask yourself the following:

- How do we make sure people understand the meaning and significance of baptism?

- How do we plan and promote our first baptism to make sure that as many people as possible attend?

- How do we capture our first baptism on video or with photography? How do we get the video or photos out to the entire church in the coming weeks?

- How do we capture the stories and testimonies of those being baptized? How do we maximize these as celebrations of what God is doing in our church family?

- How do we signify the event for those being baptized? Do we give them certificates? Framed personal photos? Group pictures?

- How do we promote a future baptism at our first baptism? (Many people, after seeing a baptism, will have

- Print out your data as hard-copy back-ups. (Sense more firsthand experience?)

- Don't let data sit around the office. Enter it immediately.

- Treat all data as confidential and proprietary.

Basic Accounting

In addition to recordkeeping and database entry, a basic accounting system is essential to running a church. Because most of us pastors are not financial wizards, we suggest finding someone you can trust to help you in this area. We are also not accountants, so what we are sharing here should not be considered bylaw for handling church funds. Make sure you seek out professional advice. But as you begin thinking through a system for accounting, some issues to get familiar with include the following:

- Offering collection, counting and deposit
- Check writing
- Reimbursement processes
- Salaries/paychecks
- Regular reports

Did your mother ever tell you to avoid all appearance of evil? You need to take that to heart and multiply it by a hundred when it comes to collecting and counting the offering and making deposits. From the very beginning, build in a solid accountability system. For example, have two individual counters sign off on the counting and place the offering in a secure envelope. Have two different people present when that envelope is opened, and then have them recount it. Once the offering is prepared for deposit, have yet another person initial the deposit slip to ensure that it matches the original count. If we sound fanatical, great! You'll never regret developing an extreme system for handling money.

On a side note, we, as pastors, never physically touch the offering. If someone wants to hand us his or her offering after the service, we walk that individual over to a staff member or volunteer who can assist him or her. When it comes to dealing with the offering, you want to stay above reproach. Granted, at the beginning you may have no choice but to handle the money yourself. If that's the case, make sure that you have an outside person present to count the money with you.

The same thinking holds true with check writing—you want to be above reproach. In the early days, you may have to write or sign checks. Don't do both. Have one person write the check and another person sign it. Make sure that there is double or triple accountability. This is especially true for reimbursement requests. You should never be the one signing on checks made payable to you. And just to make sure that we've said it, keep your personal checking account and your church checking account separate. Never, never, never mingle funds.

Paychecks are a difficult accounting issue in a new church. Dealing with taxes and withholdings can distract you from more important things! At The Journey, we have always farmed out our payroll to ADP, a reputable payroll company. Similar payroll services exist all over the country. Say hello to your first payroll department.

Finally, regular reports are a necessary part of your first-year accounting system. You will need an accurate, timely read on how much money is coming in, where it's coming from and how it's being spent. Banks are not very cooperative with new churches that go into the red! Establish accounting reports so that you always know what funds are available.

The way we as pastors do business is a testimony to those in our community. It's unacceptable for the church to bounce a check, be late depositing the offering or fail to pay the bills on time. God has called us to a higher standard in every area, but those outside the church will be more than happy to hold us accountable on this one!

Corporate/Legal Structure

In the government's eyes, churches are legal entities. We can qualify for some great benefits, like reduced postage and tax-exempt status, but these benefits do not come without proper paperwork and legal documentation. To determine what corporate or legal structure is right for your church, talk with your partner churches or your denomination. Our advice in this area is twofold:

1. Whatever corporate/legal structure you choose, make sure it's the minimum structure required. You don't want to hamper future growth of your church by having a structure that prevents you from being flexible enough to grow quickly.

2. Take your time with these issues. Don't act too quickly. Most likely, you can operate under your sponsor

church or denomination's umbrella for a period of time. Take advantage of this grace period. The only reason we listed this issue as a first-year system is so that we could warn you to go slow!

Leadership Development

Now that we've dealt with some of the more mundane first-year systems, let's look at one that's more fun! In a very real sense, the future growth of your church will be dependant on the leaders you develop. In the first year, focus your leadership development system on staff and volunteers.

Staff. From the very beginning, you will want to invest in your full-time, part-time and $50-a-week staff. Meet with them weekly. You might want to consider a regular breakfast meeting, as they may have other jobs—whatever works for everyone. During this meeting, discuss leadership books that you are all reading together (see appendix C for suggestions), and share stories of life change and encourage one another. Leadership development is really a challenge to your staff to (1) do more by raising the effectiveness and efficiency of their work, and (2) find more people to help them through the recruitment of volunteers. This simple dual focus will develop your staff both in the first year and in the years to come.

Volunteers. While you are investing in your staff, you should also be investing in your volunteers. The best investments you can make in your volunteers include the following:

- Carefully relating what is expected in every volunteer position

- Making sure volunteers understand the significance of what they are doing
- Assisting them in their spiritual growth and leadership effectiveness
- Challenging them to recruit other volunteers
- Saying "thank you" on a regular basis

As part of this system, set aside definite times throughout the first year to regularly invest in your staff and your volunteers. Trust us—it's an investment that will reap exponential results.

One Step at a Time

As we mentioned, every other system in the church outside of these eight can wait. This includes the membership class, small groups and other spiritual development processes. Let's examine why this is the case.

Why Wait on Membership Class?

Most church planters hold their first membership class way too early. We've even heard of some pastors holding a membership class before they even begin weekly services. From a systems standpoint, there is no need to expend the energy to hold membership classes until you are at least six months into weekly services. Before that time, your focus should be entirely on the monthly services, the launch and the Sunday system. From a people standpoint, you are doing a huge injustice to your people by asking them to join so early. It's in their best interests to see the church for themselves after it has started. Otherwise, they will be joining something that exists in your mind's eye, and that's dangerous.

Violate the six-month rule at your own peril. Churches that have held membership class too early have found that those who attend not only become disillusioned as the church grows but also usually end up leaving when the reality doesn't match their mental image.

Why Wait on Small Groups?

We love small groups. We are passionate about them. In fact, The Journey is known for its unique approach to small groups. Even so, we encourage you to wait at least six months before starting small groups in your new church. You may even want to wait a full year.

We waited more than six months after the time we launched The Journey to begin our small-group system. Why? Well, for starters, at the time of our launch, we didn't know people well enough to recognize good group leaders. Nor did we have enough people attending to fill up very many groups. If that weren't reason enough, we were so busy developing the essential systems that we didn't have the time or energy that would have been necessary to make our small groups successful.

It's easy to do small groups poorly, and many churches do. Usually, the small-group system suffers because the church is stretched too thin with other important activities, such as holding a Sunday service or following up with new believers. Instead of waiting until they can handle the next step of doing groups, too many churches deicide to throw the six-month-old into first grade and see how he fares.

The best rule of thumb is to wait until you have more than 65 adults in regular attendance before you start small groups, no matter how long you've been meeting (see appendix C for a recommended audio resource on small groups). In the six months between our launch and when we started small groups, we initiated several informal, temporary groups as a way of developing early relationships and identifying potential leaders for our new groups. When we did officially begin small groups, we were able to do so with seven healthy groups—and 110 people signed up (more people than had ever attended on a single Sunday!). Because we waited to start small groups, we were able to build a solid system that, to this day, involves virtually 100 percent of our weekly attendees. Good things come to those who wait.

You Get What the System Gives You

There is an old adage in systems thinking (and if you can't tell, we are quite influenced by systems thinking) that states, "The system will give you what it's designed to give you." The nervous system will give you sensation. The educational system will teach you algebra. You can't get more out of a system than it is designed to give. If you try to do too much at once in a new church, you will end up with a disjointed, anemic, struggling organism. But if you focus on building a few basic systems and build them well, you will find that your church will begin to grow, mature and soon be ready to expand. By allowing systems to do what they do, you will, in essence, move from scratch to success.

Finishing is better than starting. Patience is better than pride.

ECCLESIASTES 7:8

From Scratch to Stability to Success

Have you ever thrown an elaborate party? Remember the excitement and anticipation that came with sending out the invitations, getting your home ready for the guests, putting up decorations, setting out the finger foods and refreshments—all the while just hoping that someone would show up? The first few months of a new church feel a lot like that. That gnawing question in your gut, "Will this church really make it?" may even take a year or so to subside. But as you build your systems and begin to experience some growth, you will eventually hit a point where you realize that your young church is beginning to stabilize. Once you've made it through the critical start-up phase, you will come face to face with a whole new, completely different set of issues to keep you busy. Welcome to Phase II of your new church.

Many church planters make the mistake of slowing down as they reach the end of the start-up phase. They think they can afford to back off and relax. Huge mistake! This transition time is a key building point in the life of your church. When you see your start-up phase leveling off to stability, that's the time to accelerate your efforts to reach people and quickly break through the growth barriers that you will inevitably begin to face. It is the time to use the momentum of your start-up to your advantage.

If you back off at this point, you may never regain the excitement and speed that are helping to spur you on. You are now moving from scratch to stability and on toward long-term success. Yes, you are once again in uncharted waters. Embrace that fact, remember that God is in control, and get ready for some new adventures—the first of which will be understanding and breaking through the growth barriers that every church faces.

Breaking Growth Barriers

When it comes to moving your church forward, being proactive is the name of the game. We recommend that you make a decision right now not to let your church get stuck at any point. Learn to identify growth barriers early so that you can adjust when needed and move right through them. If you understand and know how to deal with growth barriers in advance, you will be setting yourself up for success. If you choose to be reactive rather than proactive in this area, you will constantly face the barrier battle.

The majority of churches face growth barriers at four different points: when attendance reaches 65, 125, 250 and 500. Hopefully, you will break the first growth barrier at launch and perhaps grow quickly past the second or third as well. Regardless, as you see each barrier approaching in the distance, you must make sure you are asking yourself the right questions to stay on course.

In *The Purpose Driven Church*, Rick Warren explains the wrong and right questions to ask in dealing with growth barriers:

- **The Wrong Question:** *How do I get my church to grow?* Starting with this question can lead you to wrong, even dangerous, conclusions. Here's a tip that will take a lot of pressure off you: The point of this whole endeavor is not for you to get your church to grow. You will make bad decisions when you think that growth is completely dependent on what you do or don't do. Such a mind-set often leads to pastors trying to grow their churches at any cost. If you find yourself slipping into that kind of thinking, reexamine your priorities. Remember why you became a church planter.

- **The Right Question:** *What is keeping my church from growing?* Healthy organisms grow, and that includes your church. If you feel stagnation setting in, your job is not to push growth any way you can but to identify the barriers that are hindering you and remove them.

Once you've asked this question, you must support it by making two important decisions. First, *God wants to grow your church.* You have to know beyond the shadow of a doubt that it's God's will for your church to grow, thereby expanding His kingdom. This may sound simple, but we meet a surprising number of pastors who are not convinced that God intends to grow their churches. Second Peter 3:9 teaches us, "The Lord isn't really being slow about his promise to return, as some people think. No, he is being patient for your sake. He does not want anyone to perish, so he is giving more time for everyone to repent." Do you believe that Scripture? Your new church is part of the redemptive plan He has put in place.

Some seminaries indulge a school of thought that purports just the opposite. As your new church has started to grow, you may have faced criticism from some friends. (Take note, the actual source of this criticism is often thinly veiled jealousy.) Some of you may be struggling with a casual church-growth theology. Casual theology leads to casualties in a new church. Based on the truth of Scripture and your calling, determine that it is God's will for your church to grow. Make that decision. Nail it down. God is on your side. He wants your church to grow so that His family can expand. That's why He called you.

The second important decision you must make is that *you want to see your church grow.* Maybe you believe that God wants to grow your church, but deep down, you are not willing to do what it takes to lead the charge to that next level. Does thinking about the next phase, the next barrier, drain you? Be encouraged! God will not give you a vision without supplying what you need to fulfill that vision. If you know that God called you to be a church planter, the lack of stamina you feel in leading your church on is part of the inevitable spiritual warfare you will face.

God called you to this time and this place. It wasn't so that you could give out before His job is completed. We believe that, since this book is in your hands, you are one of those pastors who will say, "Whatever it takes! I am going to do whatever it takes within God's will. I'm willing to work harder, think harder, take the next hill, and bring as many people with me as I can. God, whatever it might be, I'm willing to do it." Again, that's why He called *you.*

When you are asking the right question and you know in your core that both you and God want your church to grow for

His glory, nothing can stop you. However, growth barriers will give it their best shot. Here are the top three barriers that every growing church will face over and over again.

Growth Barrier #1: Space

Why is it that the most obvious things are sometimes the most overlooked? This is definitely the case when it comes to the number one barrier that growing churches face: the barrier of space. Maybe it's that we as pastors don't like to think about it. "Just pack 'em in," we say.

Here's the truth about space: When a room of adults reaches 70 percent of its maximum seating capacity, the room is effectively full. Period. It's time to open up additional seats or find a larger space. This is where keeping an accurate database of attendees will greatly help you. If you don't know how many people are in your room, you will not know when to take action.

Most church leaders are so happy to have a full room that they don't realize how this barrier is stalling their growth. Remember, the only people who like full rooms are preachers and worship leaders. If you ignore this barrier, your church will stop growing. Having the hard data on attendance allows you to stay ahead of this barrier and lead your church toward continued growth.

Here is a four-step exercise that you should do frequently as your church grows.

Step 1: Determine how many seats you have in your main worship space.

Step 2: Multiply that number by 70 percent.

Step 3: Determine how many people you averaged in attendance over the last month.

Step 4: Is the number in Step 3 greater than the number in Step 2?

If your answer in Step 4 is "yes," you've got to open up more seats or find a larger location—fast. Your first and easiest option is to determine whether you can comfortably put more chairs in your current space. If so, determine how many you can add and rework the exercise to see how long you can stay there.

The more difficult, but perhaps better, option is to find a larger space. If you followed our earlier advice and kept a record of all the spaces you visited while looking for an initial launch site, you can refer back to it in your search. The bottom line is that if you are out of space, it's time to move. The worst decision you can make is to wait. Use the move to build momentum in your growing church.

We learned the lesson of this growth barrier the hard way. Our first location on the Upper West Side of Manhattan was at a small comedy club-type theater called the Triad Theater. Everyone sat at round tables on Sunday mornings. The atmosphere worked well for our crowd. We liked the Triad and were in no hurry to move. Space, however, quickly became a problem. At capacity seating, the Triad could only hold 110 people. By the middle of October 2002 (just seven months after we launched), we were running close to 80 people each week. We even bumped up to 100 one Sunday! But then we dropped back down to 80—and eventually back down to near 70.

Why did our numbers drop and level off at just above 70? Because according to the barrier of space, the Triad Theater was, for all intents and purposes, full when we began averaging 77 people. That was 70 percent of the capacity. When we grew to more than 80, people consciously and subconsciously stopped inviting their friends because there was no more room. Some regular attendees even stopped coming because it was too hard to find a seat. We eventually caught on and moved to an off-Broadway theater over three times the size of the Triad. When we did, our church began growing rapidly again. Imagine that! We still regret the five months we were stalled because we stayed at the Triad too long.

Another option you might want to consider when facing this barrier is adding a second service. Multiple services are a great tool and offer your people options; however, they can be detrimental if your church is not already of a certain size. Unless you are filling a space that holds 300 or more, we recommend that you move to a larger space before adding additional services. Churches that add services when they are in smaller rooms often lose momentum because they have effectively made their gatherings feel too small. (When you do find yourself at the point of needing to add additional services, visit our website www.church fromscratch.com for some helpful resources.)

You will face the growth barrier of space at every stage of your church's development, but especially during your church's early growth. New churches grow much faster than the average church, which is why new churches should be careful about building too soon. Too many churches purchase a building or enter into a long-term lease agreement only to find themselves running out of space shortly after moving in. Early on, it's best to remain flexible. The last thing you want to do is get in a position in which God can't grow you because you aren't logistically prepared.

What if twice as many people showed up this Sunday? Would you be ready?

On a side note, church planters have a little trick when it comes to putting out extra chairs. Often, they will intentionally put out too few chairs before the service. Then, as people arrive, volunteers feverishly set up extra chairs so that everyone has a place to sit. The idea is that even if you have a small crowd, it appears larger (or at least larger than normal) because extra chairs have to be brought in. While this practice might be useful during the first monthly services, we recommend *not* doing it after the launch. Once you launch, you want to give people the impression that you are expecting them, not that you are surprised that they showed up.

Growth Barrier #2: Self-Development

The growth barrier of self-development contends that when the leadership of a church stops growing, the church stops growing. An organization of any kind cannot outgrow its leader. In *The 21 Irrefutable Laws of Leadership*, John Maxwell defines this principle as The Law of the Lid:

> If your leadership rates an 8, then your effectiveness can never be greater than a 7. If your leadership is only a 4, then your effectiveness will be no higher than a 3. Your leadership ability—for better or for worse—always determines your effectiveness and the potential impact of your organization.[1]

As one lead pastor said to us recently, "I've noticed that when I grow, the church grows." That simple statement is filled with insight. He was unwittingly talking about his own self-development, which can be defined as leadership ability plus spiritual maturity. When a lead pastor *isn't* growing:

- The church stops growing.
- The sermons are stale.
- The staff and volunteers stop growing.
- The passion for ministry wanes.

You may be familiar with Stephen Covey's *The 7 Habits of Highly Effective People*. In this record-selling book, Covey asks the reader to consider the following scenario:

Suppose you were to come upon someone in the woods working feverishly to saw down a tree.

"What are you doing?" you ask.

"Can't you see?" comes the impatient reply. "I'm sawing down this tree."

"You look exhausted!" you exclaim. "How long have you been at it?"

"Over five hours," he returns, "and I'm beat! This is hard work."

"Well, why don't you take a break for a few minutes and sharpen that saw?" you inquire. "I'm sure it would go a lot faster."

"I don't have time to sharpen the saw," the man says emphatically. "I am too busy sawing!"[2]

Can you relate to the man sawing down the tree? We can, as can most church planters and pastors. It's all too easy to neglect our own development as we try to use those very abilities to lead teams, teach people and run a successful church. However, if we don't take the time to sharpen ourselves, we will be operating at a sub-par level. We will not be as effective as God intends.

To break this growth barrier, you have to ask yourself, *What is my intentional plan for personal growth?* Self-development may take on many forms, including reading books, listening to audio recordings, or attending seminars and conferences. An intentional reading plan is one of the best avenues for self-development. We have discovered an immensely helpful reading plan that focuses on three key areas: theology, church history and philosophy. We call this plan the Triangle of Growth.

Triangle of Growth

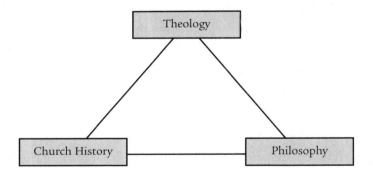

Books on theology, church history and philosophy are generally considered classics of Christian thought. The goal with this program is to read one book from each of the three areas over the course of a year. In conjunction with these more weighty books, you should also read quality Christian books or secular leadership bestsellers. We recommend reading these other types of books more quickly than those books from our reading triangle so that you will be able to spend the bulk of your reading time on the three main topics. Outline a plan for what books you are going to read in a year and then *read them*. Don't get too busy to sharpen your saw.

In addition to creating a strong reading plan, you should schedule time to attend key conferences. Our two "don't miss" conferences every year are The Purpose Driven Church Conference at Saddleback Church and the Willow Creek Leadership Summit. We also try to attend two to three more local conferences on specific leadership issues we are facing. Rick Warren once told us that you learn to grow a church to 150 people at *seminary* but you must learn to grow a church beyond that size through *seminars*. He says that each stage requires a completely different set of skills.

You may also want to consider connecting with a church coach. This could be as simple as seeking out an intensified relationship with a trusted mentor, or you could pursue a coach through an official coaching network. (For some free coaching resources and a list of the networks we recommend, visit www. churchfromsratch.com.)

Wherever your plan for self-development takes you, just make sure that you are continually on the road to becoming the best possible leader you can be. If you aren't growing yourself as a lead pastor, you won't be able to effectively lead or pastor others. Your prayer should be for God to be molding you every day into the person you need to be to lead a church twice your current size. Personal and professional development is not only essential for your own health, but it is also crucial to the growth of your church.

Growth Barrier #3: Sharing

A church will stop growing when it becomes inwardly focused—when time that was once invested in the community is now spent on maintenance concerns. When you see a decline in the number of first-time guests and an increase in discussion of inwardly focused programs, you know you are facing this growth barrier.

The growth barrier of sharing is felt more than measured, but the following ratio can prove helpful in gauging your effectiveness at bringing in first-time guests. Healthy, growing churches will have a 5 to 100 ratio of guests to attenders. In other words, an outwardly focused church will generally have five first-time guests for every 100 people in attendance. If you are averaging 200 people per week over the course of a month, then you should average 10 first-time guests each week during that same time period. We watch this ratio carefully, and if we see it begin to grow, we immediately examine whether or not we could be approaching the barrier of sharing.

When this barrier starts blocking your outreach to the community, here are some ways you can remove it:

- Teach on relational evangelism.
- Set an example by telling stories of how you've invited people to church.
- Kick off a new series with a special challenge for people to invite their friends.
- Hold a prayer walk or servant evangelism outreach.
- Talk to staff and volunteers about the importance of reaching friends.

- Read an evangelism or church-growth book with your staff.
- Develop training materials that will help your members invite their friends to church and share their faith.
- Ask someone who has experienced life change to share his or her testimony.

Be creative and confront this barrier head on! Keeping your church outwardly focused is just as important now as it was during your prelaunch stage. Make sure that you are continually working to expand God's kingdom, not building your own.

Spiritual Barriers

The growth barriers of space, self-development and sharing will be with you at every stage of your church's growth. Some may be relatively easy to break through. Others will take a lot of work. Still, while there are often technical solutions to these barriers (adding chairs, reading books, and so on), you must constantly remember that you are involved in a spiritual enterprise. The barriers you'll face stem from a spiritual battle that requires spiritual power. You, personally, have to stay plugged into the source of that power, or you will never survive. Tips and techniques will only act as band-aids, if you aren't abiding in Christ to grow you through. Remember Jesus' words in John 15:5: "I am the vine, you are the branches. He who abides in Me, and I in him, bears much fruit; for without Me you can do nothing" (*NKJV*).

With all the work that goes into starting a new church, new church planters sometimes make the fatal mistake of substituting ministry activity and professional growth for their own spiritual growth. The enemy would love to see you fall into this trap. Not only would you be operating through self-sufficiency, but you would also be cut off from the source that put you on this path to begin with. Fruit that falls away from the vine quickly dies. You need to seek the Lord's face daily in order to take on all that you will face as you seek to carry out His will.

As you move into the business of everyday church leadership, never neglect the three most important tools you have for keeping yourself in line with God.

1. *God's Word.* Carve out a time in your daily schedule to get alone with God and study His Word. Not only does Scripture make God's wisdom available to you as you face big decisions, but it also makes God's power available to you when you confront major challenges. As Hebrews 4:12 says, "For the word of God is full of living power. It is sharper than the sharpest knife, cutting deep into our innermost thoughts and desires."

2. *Prayer.* Ephesians 6:18 reminds us, "Pray at all times and on every occasion in the power of the Holy Spirit." Daily/continual prayer aligns your will with God's will and your plans with His plans. It also brings God's presence and power to bear on any situation you are facing.

3. *Fasting.* Set aside specific days to fast. Fasting centers your attention on God for the purpose of intensifying your relationship with Him. At The Journey, our entire staff

participates in day-long fasts several times throughout the year. In the past, we have fasted from solid foods for 24-hour periods as we have intensely prayed for blessing on important upcoming events (such as Easter Sunday or the kick-off of a new series) or when facing a big decision. (For more information on fasting with your staff, see our "Fasting for Spiritual Breakthrough" audio CD listed in appendix C.)

On one occasion, our church was again facing the growth barrier of space. We had run out of room, so we couldn't reach new people. Every possible lead we pursued for a new location turned into a dead end. So as a staff, we set aside several days to fast and pray for God's direction. During what would have been our meal times, and every time during the day when we felt hungry, we prayed that God would lead us to a larger worship space so that He could continue to expand His church. God answered our prayers and honored our fasting in a powerful way by providing an incredible space for us. Sometimes it takes fasting! Jesus told us in Mark 9:29, "This kind [of demon] can be cast out by prayer and fasting."

Starting Other Churches

One of the driving passions behind the concept of launching large is that it allows a church to reproduce more quickly. When a church stays small for many years or never really reaches a point of stability, it simply is not capable of birthing other churches. Just as a 10-year-old child is not ready to become a parent, a church that is still dependent on outside support is not ready to start new healthy churches. However, once a church is fully financed by its members and attendees, it's time to consider starting additional churches.

Ingrain into the DNA of your early church the desire to eventually start new churches. Cast that vision. Make sure your people know that your church will eventually start other churches, both locally and around the world. In your post-launch budget, determine to set aside at least a small amount of money to assist in starting churches, even if it's only $50 or $100 per month. Plant the seeds. Mobilize early mission teams to work with new churches in your area or on national mission trips. Remind your people that you are a new church (some people who come in a year or two after your launch may not be aware of your history) and that you are committed to helping other churches.

Here are three great ways for your growing church to move toward starting another church:

1. *Find a church planter inside your church.* New churches often raise up other planters quickly. Be on the lookout for people who might have this desire and calling. Give them resources and take them to conferences with you.

2. *Find a church planter who is moving to your area.* If there's already a solid church planter in your region, seek out a partnership. If there's a good match, jump in as one of their financial partners.

3. *Find out where your current financial partners are working and join them.* The churches that helped you financially may have other partnerships that they are pursuing. If they are doing something that ignites your passion, get on board.

Earnestly seek God's will here so that you don't fall into the common trap of dualistic thinking. Too many growing churches that consider starting other churches end up asking themselves, *Is it God's will for us to grow larger or for us to plant other churches?* This is not an either/or proposition. God can fully intend for you to do both. We call this "bifocal vision": keeping one eye on the growth and health of your church and one eye on planting other churches.

As a model for starting other churches, look to the guideline in Acts 1:8: "You will receive power and will tell people about me everywhere—in Jerusalem, throughout Judea, in Samaria, and to the ends of the earth." Then lay out a three-to-five-year plan for planting churches in each mentioned area:

- Locally (Jerusalem)
- Regionally (throughout Judea)
- Nationally/cross culturally (in Samaria)
- Globally (to the ends of the earth)

Keep the Dream Alive

As your church moves beyond the start-up phase, set aside some time to do an activity we call "The Next Five Years." Fast forward your mind five years into the future and ask yourself, *With God's lead, what will our church look like in five years?* Take time to dream about the following:

- What if our attendance doubles, triples or more over the next few years?
- What if our current monthly giving amount becomes our weekly giving?
- What if our current yearly budget becomes our monthly budget?
- What if our small groups were 2 to 10 times larger?
- What if we had 2 to 10 times the first-time guests we have now?
- What if we had 2 to 10 times the children/youth that we have now?
- What would our staff look like if we were two to three times bigger?
- What if God interrupted this planning and did more than we could imagine?

Never stop dreaming God's dream for your church.

The Final Challenge

Here is our final challenge to you: Be a church that constantly gives back to other churches for the greater good of the Kingdom. If your new church has experienced healthy growth, you undoubtedly understand that it is evidence of God at work and not anything you can take credit for. Let your passion to glorify God stir you to be a good steward of the resources, ideas and dollars He has entrusted to you.

As you consider giving back resources, ask, "What resources have helped my church grow the most?" Maybe there are books you could recommend to other pastors who are starting churches (hopefully this will be one of them!). Perhaps there are conferences, training materials or internal forms or documents that you could share with other pastors.

As you consider giving back ideas, ask, "What have I learned that has most impacted the health and growth of my church?" Ideas are more valuable than money. Capture your ideas on paper and share them with other pastors over lunch or at informal gatherings. Ideas are the currency of God's kingdom.

As you consider giving back dollars, ask, "How would God have us invest our financial resources to help other churches?" This could be through helping to start churches locally, regionally, nationally and globally, or you may be led to support your denomination or a similar mission agency. Old sayings become old sayings because they are true, and this one definitely is: "You can't outgive God!" God will bless you as you bless others.

The greatest churches in the world are yet to be launched. Over the next decade, we will see churches launch large, reach the unchurched, grow people to maturity in Christ, and start new churches at an unprecedented rate. There is no better time in history to start a church from scratch than right now! Welcome to the adventure.

Go therefore and make disciples of all the nations.

MATTHEW 28:19, *NKJV*

Notes

1. John Maxwell, *The 21 Irrefutable Laws of Leadership* (Nashville, TN: Thomas Nelson Publishers, 1998), p. 1.
2. Stephen Covey, *The 7 Habits of Highly Effective People* (New York: Simon and Schuster, 1989), p. 287.

We hope this book will become a conversation starter between us and you. We are constantly developing resources and gathering ideas to help churches reach their full redemptive potential, whether they're brand-new churches or great existing churches. To help facilitate this conversation, we have set up a website where you will find helpful tools as well as the option to discuss the book directly with us and/or other practitioners. We would love to hear your story and help you through the process of launching your church. The website address is: **www.ChurchFromScratch.com.**

Your partners in ministry,

Nelson and Kerrick

Also Available

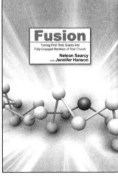

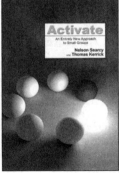

Fusion:
How to Keep More First-Time Guests
Nelson Searcy with Jennifer Henson
ISBN 08307.45319
Available 1/2/08

Activate:
An Entirely New Approach to Small Groups
Nelson Searcy with Kerrick Thomas
ISBN 08307.45661
Available 6/2/08

Average Monthly Attendance for the First Two Years of The Journey

(April 2002 – March 2004)

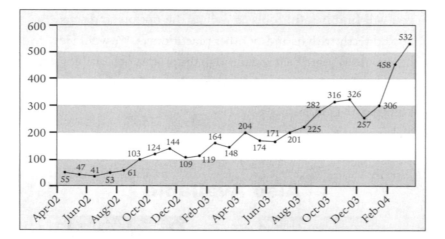

Year #1 at The Journey:		Year #2 at The Journey:	
April 2002:	55	April 2003:	204
May 2002:	47	May 2003:	174
June 2002:	41	June 2003:	171
July 2002:	53	July 2003:	201
August 2002:	61	August 2003:	225
September 2002:	103	September 2003:	282
October 2002:	124	October 2003:	316
November 2002:	144	November 2003:	326
December 2002:	109	December 2003:	257
January 2003:	119	January 2004:	306
February 2003:	164	February 2004:	458
March 2003:	148	March 2004:	532